THE
PRACTICAL**PREACHER**
practical wisdom for the pastor-teacher

EDITED**BY**
WILLIAM**PHILIP**

contributions by:
MELVIN**TINKER** • DAVID**JACKMAN** • MARTIN**ALLEN**
JONATHAN**PRIME** • SINCLAIR**FERGUSON**

Foreword

There are welcome signs in many parts of the world today of a recovery of biblical preaching, and this emphasis is substantially due to the dedicated work of the Proclamation Trust.

The five contributors to this book are all Proclamation Trust conference speakers, and are together committed to the supreme authority of the Bible and to the primacy of its exposition in the Church.

The Practical Preacher is well named, for its authors are mature pastors who are able to share with us from their experience. They give valuable advice on such issues as how to commend Biblical exposition to a congregation unaccustomed to it; how to plan sermon series; and how to treat our hearers as real people. They also give practical wisdom on a sermon's theme and aim, structure and language, illustration and application.

Not that they limit themselves to practical questions; they also have important things to say about the relations between preaching, pastoral care and theology.

Because I share these authors' conviction that the church lives by the Word of God and languishes without it, I gladly commend their book to all preacher-pastors.

John Stott
June 2002

Contents

Introduction

Not only was the Teacher wise, but also he imparted knowledge to the people.
(Eccl. 12:9)

The primary work of the pastor must be that of teaching the word of God. But there is a great deal more to being a pastor-teacher than simply having the ability to preach. Clearly this gifting is foundational, for the New Testament makes clear that the chief means of shepherding – pastoring – the flock of God is through the teaching and application of all the Scriptures in the church. God has not left his people helpless in the face of the trials of life, but in giving the church the word of God in Scripture he has given us everything we need for life and godliness (2 Pet. 1:3). And the Chief Shepherd himself has given to his church under-shepherds with the task of ministering this word in all its fullness, calling and gifting them by his Holy Spirit to enable them to serve his church in this way.

But even a cursory reading of the pastoral epistles, or the letters of Peter or James, must alert us to the fact that we can never take the teaching, far less the mere ability to teach, in isolation. There is so much space devoted by the apostles to the responsibilities of leadership in Christ's church, and to the qualifications for such leadership, that we are forced to recognise that what is taught cannot be divorced from he who teaches. Indeed, as we read these letters, we are struck by how closely the spotlight focuses upon the life and doctrine of the teacher, and how little discussion there is of actual teaching ability *per se*. Although it is taken for granted that the teacher will be 'apt to teach' (2 Tim. 2:24), frankly all the emphasis falls on what is to be taught, and the character of the one who teaches it. The apostles are very concerned not only that the church receives teaching that is in 'the pattern of sound [apostolic] teaching', but that it is ministered 'with faith and love in Christ Jesus' (2 Tim. 1:13). Let us put it another way: for those of us who are ministers of the word of God, it is not just what we teach, but how we teach and what we ourselves are as we teach that matters greatly to our Lord, and to his church.

How we approach with godly wisdom the whole task of being a pastor-teacher in Christ's church, then, should exercise us greatly. This is why, no doubt, there is a whole division of study in the academy called 'practical theology'. But the problem is that many a student finds the things taught under that discipline embrace precious little theology, and then discovers in his experience as a pastor that there is not much that could be construed as practical either! This predicament stems largely from the fact that too few of those training ministers seem to have a biblical definition of what ministry in the church of God really is. They do not recognise the primacy of the pastoral task of teaching, and therefore divorce all that is to do with pastoring (which is largely psychologised) from all that is to do with teaching (which is often ignored altogether). The danger for eager ministers committed to the primacy of a preaching ministry is that, out of frustration with this state of affairs, we may throw out the baby with the bath-water, becoming dismissive of the need for any kind of practical theology at all. 'All we need do is preach the word!' we say. Well, we must preach the word; but if we take seriously the New Testament injunctions abou[...] we address this primary pastoral task, we will show our wi[...] by humility, a teachable spirit and diligence in pursuing all profitable means so as to present ourselves as approved and unashamed workmen of God (2 Tim. 2:15).

This little book has not got all the answers, but we hope it may help with some of them. Each contribution comes from someone who is committed to the belief that the primary pastoral task is the ministry of the word of God, and each has experience in local church ministry, though the length of that experience varies. The focus of the book is therefore on the preaching ministry, hence the title. But the aim is that by dealing with differing facets of what is involved in authentic expository ministry, there may be real practical help for those seeking to pursue and develop such a ministry. There is inevitably some overlap between chapters, but this serves to emphasise where different contributors have come to the same conclusions about ministry through quite separate experience.

Throughout, there is a twin focus which keeps emerging as of great importance: the pastor, and the people. These two, the relationship between them and the knowledge one of the other, are intimately related and inextricable. The wise teacher will, we trust, learn something from the exploration of them in this book. It is about real pastors, real people and real ministry. The truly wise teacher is the one who, by having a biblically earthed knowledge of such things, is a real pastor who imparts real knowledge of God to real people.

We are very grateful to all the contributors who have allowed the material to be edited from recordings of addresses given at various recent conferences of The Proclamation Trust, with very little personal involvement. Any deficiencies, therefore, must be laid solely at the door of the editor.

WJUP
The Proclamation Trust
Spring 2002

List of Contributors

Melvin Tinker is minister of St John's, Newland Church of England in Hull, and was previously Anglican chaplain of Keele University.

David Jackman has been the Director of The Proclamation Trust's Cornhill Training Course since 1991, and prior to that was minister of Above Bar Church in Southampton.

Martin Allen is minister of Chryston Church of Scotland, near Glasgow, where he has ministered for over twenty years.

Jonathan Prime is minister of Enfield Evangelical Free Church in north London.

Sinclair Ferguson is minister of St George's Tron Church of Scotland in Glasgow, and was formerly Professor of Systematic Theology at Westminster Theological Seminary, Philadelphia.

1

Preparing a Congregation for Expository Preaching

Melvin Tinker

Many younger evangelical ministers, especially those in mixed denominations, increasingly find themselves beginning ministry in non-evangelical settings. Some seem to think that it is possible to get from a Little Puddleton-on-the-Marsh to an All Souls, Langham Place in about two months. This is not terribly realistic! So how, under God, does one realistically begin to turn the church around through the ministry of the word? Others find themselves in church planting situations, where the majority will not be used to any preaching of any kind. So how can we wean our congregation on to good solid food?

I am not claiming to have all the answers of course, or that I have always got it right. Far from it. But in an effort to stimulate creative thinking among others, let me share with you some of the principles involved, and how they might actually work out in practice in ordinary church life. We must begin with Scripture which enunciates the basic principles we need to apply in order to achieve the goal of biblical expository ministry in our churches.

Paul sent to Ephesus for the elders of the church. [18] When they arrived, he said to them: 'You know how I lived the whole time I was with you, from the first day I came into the province of Asia. [19] I served the Lord with great humility and with tears, although I was severely tested by the plots of the Jews. [20] You know that I have not hesitated to preach anything that would be helpful to you but have taught you publicly and from house to house. [21] I have declared to both Jews and Greeks that they must turn to God in repentance and have faith in our Lord Jesus.
(Acts 20:17-21)

Let me suggest that this pattern, drawn from the life of the apostle Paul, ought to provide a practical guide when we find ourselves beginning a new ministry in a situation where expository word ministry is fairly new, or perhaps treated with a good deal of suspicion. Let us first try to summarise some of the principles here, before unpacking things further.

Key principles drawn from Paul's pattern of ministry

1. Ministry takes place within a particular context (v.17), here for Paul in the province of Asia. It is important that we do take on board the fact that contexts vary, and that these will tend to shape the manner of word ministry.

2. Expository word ministry does not occur in a vacuum. It is related to the rest of our lives and the lives of the people to whom we minister. Paul says here, 'you know how I lived the whole time I was with you' (v.18). The time reference there may

also be significant, because three years was a relatively long haul for Paul as a missionary apostle. It is well-grounded ministry which lasts. More and more we do need long-stay ministers who produce enduring evangelical churches.

3. Expository word ministry is more than pulpit or public ministry: 'I taught you publicly and from house to house' (v.20b).

4. It will involve very hard work, will be emotionally draining, and can only be carried out in a spirit of utter dependence upon God. Indeed there will be times when we will feel wholly inadequate for the task. Paul says here, 'I served the Lord with great humility and with tears' (v.19). Some of those tears may well be shed for those who will walk away from such ministry; it will break our hearts but we have got to expect it.

5. There will be opposition: 'I was severely tested by the plots of the Jews'(v.19b).

6. It will involve a comprehensive handling of Scripture, concerned with the wellbeing of the congregation. Paul did not shrink back from teaching anything that would be helpful (20); he did not shrink from declaring the whole counsel of God (v.27).

7. Finally, at the heart of all exposition is not entertainment but the gospel. This alone has power to change lives and bring men and women into a living relationship with the one true God. In other words, we must never lose our evangelical focus: 'I declared to both Jews and Greeks that they must turn to God in repentance and have faith in our Lord Jesus Christ' (v.21).

There is a very great deal that could be said on each of these seven points. We shall have to keep them in mind as we explore the issues in more detail, with a particular practical focus on local church ministry.

Expository preaching must be sensitive to the church context

First of all is this question of context. While being wholly committed to expository word ministry, the way we engage in that ministry will vary to a lesser or greater degree depending upon our context. When I arrived at St John's Newland (an Anglican church in Hull) just over six years ago, it would have been described as a broad or liberal evangelical church, some would say 'vaguely evangelical'. Expository preaching was certainly not its hallmark. Within that church there were essentially three separate congregations. There was a small 8am holy communion service, using the Book of Common Prayer, and mainly consisting of elderly people. Then, there was a 10.30am service which was medium sized, just a little over the hundred mark. It was mainly composed of families, though with few children, and a wide cross section of ages and background. There were no students at that stage. There was also a small 6.30pm service, which perhaps had the greatest potential for reaching students. We are right next door to Hull University and Humberside University, and both are within our parish.

So we were faced with three different contexts in terms of the congregation. But this also has to be placed within the wider context of the area in which St John's finds itself. It is a mixed area: urban priority area (UPA) housing on the one hand, through to some very large houses with swimming pools on the other. And this in turn has got to be placed within an even larger context of a city which has the lowest church attendance of any city in the UK. We also have great problems with children; for example, teenage pregnancy is very high. So, inevitably, all this is going to affect the shape of the public expository ministry.

Initially in entering this situation, these factors will determine the length of sermon in all three services. You may not particularly like that, and you may think it is letting the side down! But I have to say that it is good to start off short. Working over a period of time to more substantial lengths, one must allow the congregation to get used to preaching, and to acquire the repertoire to cope with it. Hopefully, in God's grace, they will also develop the taste to desire it. So with the 8am service, in our case, that meant just giving a ten to fifteen minute sermon, majoring on one point with a good deal of application. Bearing in mind it is an elderly congregation, we want illustrations that will link in with their experience. No use pretending they are students just because we fancy ourselves as having a student ministry! With the 10.30am service, the sermon started off as twenty minutes, and similarly with the 6.30pm—the application and the illustrations chosen to be appropriate to the group concerned. The preaching is much longer than that now, but that is how we began.

Now when you think about it, all this is applying the scriptural principle of feeding with milk and then with meat. It also means ensuring that the basics of the gospel are taught regularly and in a varied and interesting fashion. Many in the church will be 'nominal' Christians. Others will be true believers, but perhaps starved of Bible teaching, and their faith needs reawakening and strengthening. Still others will be there who are knowingly non-Christians; in our case, for instance, people come for the reading of banns of marriage. Richard Baxter's book, *The Reformed Pastor,* is in itself an exposition of Acts 20. It is a mine of good advice, and on this point he writes:

> The work of conversion, of repentance from dead works and of faith in Christ, must be taught first and in a frequent and thorough manner. The stewards of God's household must give to each their portion in due season. We must never go beyond the capacities of our people, nor should we teach Christian maturity to those who have not yet learned the

first lesson. Augustine says, 'An infant is nourished according to its strength. It will be able to take more as it grows. But if we exceed what a babe is able to take, then its strength will decrease rather than increase'.

The question of context will also have a deciding influence on the type of sermon series we opt for, and we shall come back to this later.

Expository ministry is part of a shared life

The second point related to context is that word ministry does not operate in a vacuum. In order to make sure that we engage properly with the members of our congregation in our teaching, and to establish confidence in what we are doing, we need time to get to know them. In the early days of ministry this does mean a lot of visiting, especially the key members of the church: the elders or members of the church council, and as many others as possible. Whatever we like to think, the fact is that if we are locked away in our study most of the day in sermon preparation right at the beginning, then the complaints will come in thick and fast. People will say that their minister is rather aloof, that they do not really know him, that he does not care. This is especially so if you replace a minister who majored on pastoral visiting. Invariably you will be compared, and in an unfavourable way.

So, strategic visiting in the first few months can offset this a good deal. For a start you will be able to listen to what their hopes and fears are for the church. When a new minister arrives in a church people get rather twitchy: 'What is he going to do?' they will be saying. Well, hear what their hopes and fears are, as well as sharing with them your hopes and fears, your vision for the church. For them to see the minister's human face is very important, and of course that is what Paul did, as he reminds us here in Acts 20 and in 1 Thessalonians. He shared his life with his people; he was not just tucked away in a study, but out there among them.

So how does all this square with wanting to produce good sermons, which invariably require a lot of time to prepare? Well, to let you into the secret, for the first year or so I used sermons that I had preached elsewhere. This is a wise thing to do because you can spend more time in visiting during the first six months. Then, as people begin to respond to the expository ministry, you can explain that the sermons take time to produce. By then they have a greater level of trust to take you at your word because they think they know you. Hopefully they do! I would also want to recommend that we do take the opportunity from the pulpit, as well as privately, to explain this to people. I often see people's jaws drop when I tell them just how long it takes me to prepare each sermon. You can see the look of shock and horror on their face!

Let me give an example of this. Recently we had a sermon series on the church and one sermon was on the nature of ministry. In this sermon I was expounding Acts 20 under the title 'Crooks and Shepherds' and I said the following to the congregation:

> With Paul we must proclaim the whole will of God to the whole people of God. That is why we value what's called expository preaching here at St John's; that is, to work through a book or a passage and to let the Bible speak for itself. We try to parcel it out over the course of a year, so we cover Old Testament, Gospels, Letters and major doctrines and matters of Christian living which we face today. That way you can see it is the word and not the world that sets the agenda. The world raises certain questions, 'Why is there suffering?' but God

too wants to raise with us his questions, 'Why are you so rebellious? Why don't you recognise the utter folly of living without me and come to know the truth in my Son and then you will be free?' And that's what Paul is saying here: turn to God in repentance and faith in Jesus.

Now let me ask by way of extending this principle, those of you who are husbands, how are you encouraging your family to understand and apply the word of God? When you watch the television together or you have a meal together, do you say 'Well let's just think about what we've heard or watched from a Christian viewpoint?' How proactive are you as a parent or a grandparent in getting God's truth into your children's and your grandchildren's life? Buy them that book which will help or that tape with a good message. Encourage them along to Sunday School. Show by your own example that you take it seriously. Do they ever catch you reading a Bible or Christian book? You see publicly and from house to house, Paul made it his aim to teach the whole will of God and surely our aim should not be anything less.

That was a simple word of explanation of what we do, to the congregation and to many newcomers also, as well as giving some pointed application. But hopefully, after a period of time, the people will see that this is what lies at the heart of our ministry.

Additionally, meeting folk helps to earth the sermons in real lives so that people will know that we know what we are talking about, that we have not just dug these up from our bookshelves, that we do not just live a cloistered existence. Some call this walking the shop floor. Obviously how we operate will vary according to our temperament and our own situation. Personally, I work best in the mornings and that is why I devote those mornings to sermon preparation. After six years people know that is what I do and they have learnt not to try and disturb me in the mornings. Afternoons and evenings tend to be freer for visiting. But of course we have got to be flexible, as was the apostle Paul.

Expository preaching is part of a wider culture of word ministry

But a word ministry does not operate in a vacuum in another sense, namely in relation to the whole life of the church and especially what can be called public worship. In this area small changes might have to be made initially which will enhance the ministry of the word. For example, it may be very simple, but quite important, to start the service on time. When I arrived at St John's, services tended to start about fifteen minutes after they should have started, because the minister would come in late or there would be notices which would go on forever and ever. So, just to start at bang-on the appointed time of 10.30am made a big difference. Or again, a simple thing like reducing the number of notices can be a huge help. We have a notice sheet and only highlight one or two. Choose hymns that will actually reinforce the theme of the text, and people will eventually say, 'Ah, yes, I can see how it all ties together.' Choose only good people who can read the Bible publicly (if that is what you do), and have pew Bibles and encourage their use. You will find that if the rest of the service runs well, people will be all the more ready to listen to the sermon, as you make more time for it and give it a central place. So in that sense, too, it does not take place in a vacuum.

Of course word ministry is more than pulpit ministry, although this should be where the lion's share of our time and devotion will go. But it will be enhanced if we can see our preaching as part of developing the church's wider appreciation of God's word in shaping its life and witness. This may be introduced initially in very small ways: the short devotional talk before a church leadership meeting, incorporating a sermon in the parish magazine, developing Bible based Sunday schools (which means taking time to train the leaders), establishing growth or home groups, seeking out people who seem interested in the Bible and targeting them, and so on. One of the very first things I did was to form a men's Bible study on a Saturday morning once a month. Just a few men who did seem to be interested got together and then it snowballed. Getting the Bible into the women's programmes is also vital. That is not always easy by any means, especially where such programmes are flower arranging and anything but the Bible; but eventually to get the Bible into their programmes is a very positive thing. When you go visiting, at least leave with a short Bible reading and prayer. In counselling let it be biblical wisdom that is evident, and so on. These are all small things but they have a cumulative effect.

Then of course there is the matter of extending people's interest. Maybe you can share some good tapes with a few key people. Perhaps invite the occasional good visiting preacher, so that they realise that this is not just their pastor's peculiarity, his way of doing ministry; other people are doing it like this as well. Show how important the preaching is by encouraging folk to read through the passages before next Sunday, and perhaps reinforce what is preached with sermon outlines for people to take away (we produce these for every sermon).

In all these ways people will see that you take preaching seriously and therefore they should take it seriously too. They will realise that we are working hard for them and that is why we want to encourage them to work hard together. What it boils down to is developing a whole culture of word ministry, a total environment in which it can operate.

Expository ministry is a costly ministry

We must be prepared for the hard work and the emotional cost as well as the opposition. A few years ago John Chapman was at a Theological Students conference and he asked the students this question: 'Are you willing to put in the hard yards?' He pointed out that it is relatively easy to do that if you are at a large church with a large number of eager listeners, but what about if you are faced with smaller numbers and those who are less than willing to listen? Then, of course, it is much harder to do. In terms of preparation a lot more thought and care is required when you are up against either an ignorant or an unwilling congregation. It is a greater challenge to wield the sword of the Spirit a little more skilfully to hit the target. There will be hours of reading and praying and writing. There will be the emotional waste you feel on Sunday evening, 'the preacher's fainting fits' as Spurgeon used to call them. I certainly have had times when I have almost had to physically drag myself up into the pulpit because I felt unable and, to my shame, unwilling to do it. But that is when you do feel that dependence upon God. It is not a nice feeling, but ultimately it is a good one.

I have found John Piper's advice quite helpful here. Some of you may have come across this acronym before: APTAT – Admit your need, pray to God, trust he's heard you, act and then thank. I find myself doing that before every sermon now. One other thing I have found helpful is the one year, five year rule:

> Do not overestimate what you do in one year
> and do not underestimate what can be achieved
> in five years.

When I went to St John's I gave myself five years before I was going to see any significant change – man of little faith! We saw change more rapidly, but this is not a bad maxim to aim for.

Do not overestimate what you can do in one year, do not underestimate what can be achieved in five years.

But we can expect opposition. It may not be as intense as that which Paul experienced, but it can be just as real, often taking the form of a few well placed jibes about your sermons, even though you have only preached for ten minutes. Again the words of Baxter,

> We must bear with many abuses and injuries from those for whom we are doing good. When we have studied their case, prayed with them and besought and exhorted them, and spent ourselves for them, we still need more patience with them. We can still expect that after we have looked upon them as our own children that there may be some who will reject us with scorn, even hate and contempt. God may yet lead them to repentance. Even when they scorn and reject our ministry and tell us to mind our business yet we must still persevere in caring for them, for we are dealing with distracted people who will reject their physician. Nevertheless we must persist with their cure, he is indeed an unworthy doctor who would be driven away simply by the foul language of the patient.

It does hurt when people disappoint us, especially those who at the outset seemed to be the most promising supporters. When these walk away, one can get very low. But this too, must be expected. It happened to Paul, and it happened to our Lord himself; it will happen to us if we are faithful to their message.

Expository preaching m
long-term purpose

What of the shape and content of the
ministry itself? Well, as we saw with
comprehensive in scope and it must have the
welfare in view. We are not there to impress peo   seek
their accolades; we are to benefit them spiritually. A   i venture
to share with you a few practical pointers that I found helpful in
the first few years of ministry, and which aim to produce a long
lasting expository ministry, not just a transient one.

Let us consider sermon series. Many people are biblically
illiterate and even basic Bible stories cannot be taken for granted
any longer, especially among younger people. It is therefore vitally
important to enable people to get familiar with the whole Bible
as quickly as possible, as well as becoming aware of basic
Christian truths. I think this means going for short series and
having a programme which covers a wide range of material –
Old Testament, New Testament, Gospels, narrative, prophecy,
epistles and so on. That will help them not to be afraid of
turning to the Bible themselves, because it is to them uncharted
territory. Our job is to help them to chart the territory so that
they realise that the whole Bible is interesting and supremely
relevant.

This is the pattern I adopted in the first year of arriving in
my present situation. On Sunday mornings in the first term, I
covered some basic material on the Trinity, on the grandeur of
God. (I felt that you have really got to work hard to mess up
Isaiah 40, opening people's eyes to the wonder of this God!)
Then, we turned to the question 'Who is Jesus?' using that great
hymn from Philippians 2, and subsequently moved on to the
Holy Spirit. Then, because in a new situation I wanted people to
try and understand what the church is all about, we had a short
series on the Master's plan for the church: heavenly church, gifted
church, witnessing church, caring church, giving chu

church and so on.

the evening we started off covering things people would feel comfortable with: a short series on the Psalms, then Luke's Gospel. Most of these had an evangelistic focus and so there were evangelistic guest services. Then, being an Anglican church, in celebrating Advent three things came up on judgement. In the second term we looked at various episodes from John's Gospel, called 'Close Encounters'. [1] Once again, this was to open people's eyes and to get the gospel across. We moved on to discipleship, to some basic things on prayer and, coming up to Easter, three sermons on the resurrection. From there we moved on to a series on the Ten Commandments, and so on in a similar way.

Expository preaching must be relevant to the contemporary world

It is probably true to say that in many people's minds, if they have heard of the term, expository preaching means boring verse-by-verse Bible study. True expository preaching is not that, and therefore we do need to work extra hard to make contact between the world and the word, and to make that contact as obvious and as stimulating as possible. I have found that this means working very hard at introductions and endings to sermons. I spend a disproportionate amount of time getting the introduction right in order to try to capture the minds of the hearers. Sometimes I start with some issue that is pressing, and then work from the text to show how it deals with it. Throughout the sermon there has to be constant application, flowing between the word and the world. This sort of n has to be going on in order that our application and y is engaging. It is important to have the congregation eye in preparing the sermon. What is the make-up itual-wise, background-wise? That will help to

d under that title by Christian Focus Publications.

shape the application and illustration. This is where walking the shop floor is vital; we get to know the people to whom we are ministering and therefore we can target the word accordingly.

Try to ensure that you do preach the occasional topical sermon series, but do still deal with it expositionally: teaching a passage or a number of passages that deal with an issue. I say that because I have been finding that even after six years, even good people are not thinking Christianly; they are still being shaped by the values of the world, to which they are far more exposed than the values of the word. We must not take anything for granted. We cannot assume anymore that even Christians think sex before marriage is wrong, or that children should be disciplined, or that Christ is the only way of salvation, or that divorce is evil (even though sometimes we may think it is the lesser of two evils). Recently I devised a sermon series entitled, 'By the Rivers of Babylon – living Christianly in today's world', the idea being we are like a church in captivity. We need to deal with idolatry, questions of morality, marriage, questions of work, sexuality and raising children. But we need to do so expositionally, that is, clearly and coherently from the pages of Scripture. So, this series was aimed at a mixed congregation, of blue collar and white collar workers, young and old, and it was very well received. I think people can take a lot more than we give them credit for. It is not only students who can think!

It is like serving up a meal: variety is the spice of life. I would argue that the days of extremely long sermon series are by and large gone for most of us, at least in the early days of a new ministry. But we do certainly want people to get hold of the whole Bible books. Shorter books are easily managed; with longer books samples might be used, taking passages which perhaps are key to the book's structure and development. They can be divided into parts, term one doing one part, term three doing the second part. I think the key is to keep it fresh and varied and that way we keep ourselves on our toes and go to books we would normally shy away from.

Expository preaching must be rooted in the biblical gospel

Finally, as Acts 20:20 reminds us, we must have a gospel focus. This involves two points. First, we must preach evangelistically through exposition. It is not the only way to preach evangelistically, but I do want to recommend it as the method we use the most often. Take a passage in which the gospel is unpacked, and preach it in context. This allows the word to set the agenda and demonstrates both to Christians and non-Christians the power and the relevance of Scripture. It is often great at subverting and overturning people's expectations of Christianity. 'I didn't realise that's what the Bible said!' It also helps non-Christians to follow the reasoning because they have the passage before them, preferably in a Bible or even printed out on sheets. It shows that it is God addressing us through the Bible rather than the preacher's blessed thoughts. God is the primary speaker.

Secondly, as we preach from around the Bible, and pay heed to the different genres, we demonstrate that the whole of the Bible is able to make us wise to salvation. We demonstrate the belief that there is only one author, the Holy Spirit, one central character, the Lord Jesus Christ, and one theme which is the kingdom of God and the salvation that is to be found in Christ. God's word is a unified word. Expository preaching proceeds on this assumption and demonstrates it most clearly. It begins to excite people as they discover that the same gospel is there in Isaiah and the book of Ruth as in John's Gospel and Romans. It also ensures that preaching does not become dull and stagnant. Most of all it brings glory to God, because this is the method by which he has chosen to reveal himself to us.

2

Planning a Preaching Programme

David Jackman

In the previous chapter, Melvin Tinker drew attention to Acts 20 in which we have one of the clearest accounts of apostolic ministry in the New Testament. We shall inevitably revisit some of the same ground in this chapter, though the particular focus will be on a more detailed look at planning an ongoing programme for preaching and teaching throughout congregational life, rather than just at the beginning of a new ministry. But let us remind ourselves just how instructive Paul is as he describes his longest settled ministry at Ephesus in this passage of Scripture. From what he says, we can piece together the ingredients of what he thought was important in his preaching programme while he was there.

First, Paul was concerned that everything he did would be helpful (v.20). He wanted to preach in such a way that they were helped by his preaching. It sounds obvious, but of course it is possible to preach in such a way that this is not primary. You simply air the bees that are in your bonnet or share the illumination that you yourself happen to have received recently. But the congregation gives a very important focus to Paul's preaching:

he wants his preaching to be helpful – in the teaching sessions within the church gathering at Ephesus, and also in his house-to-house ministry.

Second, at the heart of Paul's preaching programme is the gospel, and preaching the gospel as the grace of God. He 'declared ... repentance and faith' (v.21) in order to be faithful to his calling of 'testifying to the gospel of God's grace' (v.24). It is important to ask ourselves, how much of our preaching programme is characterised by preaching God's grace? For example, it is terribly easy to preach something like the Sermon on the Mount as a new law rather than preaching it as grace. And an integral part of preaching the gospel is preaching not only forgiveness and restoration, but also the Lordship and the kingly rule of Christ, preaching the kingdom (v.25).

Paul sums up his preaching ministry by saying that what he 'has not hesitated to proclaim' is 'the whole counsel of God' (v.27, KJV). Everything that God has revealed of his mind and will is what he has proclaimed. It is a striking compression of the priorities of apostolic ministry – preaching anything that would be helpful, declaring the gospel of God's grace, calling to repentance and faith, preaching the kingly rule of Christ, proclaiming the whole will of God. We would all sign up to this, no doubt. So, ask yourself the question: what have you been doing in the last six months? How does it measure up to the Pauline priorities? Because, according to Paul, this is the only way the church will be defended and built up:

> Keep watch over yourselves and all the flock of which the Holy Spirit has made you overseers. Be shepherds of the church of God which he bought with his own blood, for I know that after I leave savage wolves will come in among you and will not spare the flock. Even from your own number men will arise and distort the truth in order to try to draw

disciples away after them, so be on your guard.
(Acts 20:28)

This is why it is so important to have a preaching programme
with these priorities, to proclaim the whole will of God, to
preach anything that is helpful – helpful in defending the flock,
guarding it from false teachers , from savage wolves and from
those that arise from within the church distorting the truth. There
is going to be constant distortion, and this must be counteracted
by faithful preaching and constant warning not to be drawn
away after that error, but to stand firm in the truth, to be on
your guard. But in the midst of all this, there is also great assurance:

> Now I commit you to God and to the word
> of his grace which can build you up and give
> you an inheritance among all those who are
> sanctified.
> (Acts 20:32)

That is the confidence. The preaching programme is all about
the word of his grace, which does the work, which can build
you up and give you an inheritance: build you up in this life,
keep you persevering to heaven and give you that inheritance
amongst all who are sanctified.

SETTING PRIORITIES

Such was Paul's agenda for Ephesus when he was there, and so
he commissions the elders to follow in his footsteps and to plan
their preaching programmes around those priorities. This is laying
the foundation for all that follows, because if these priorities
are not there then whatever programme we produce, it will be
ineffective. If the flock is going to be fed, defended, nurtured,
strengthened, then these are the priorities and we must have that

31

...s the word of God, in the hands of the Spirit
...oes the work of God.

...o New Testament Christianity is this concept, that
...ion-negotiable body of truth which needs to be taught,
...iich needs to be learned – not simply in an intellectual or
propositional way, but even more importantly in a relational
way. The Lord Jesus said that life eternal is 'to know you, the
only true God and Jesus Christ whom you have sent' (John
17:3). That relational knowledge with God is the purpose of
Scripture. If our preaching programme is built on the word of
God's grace, then that grace brings us into relationship with
him, and at the heart of our preaching programme there has to
be not simply the conveying of propositional truth, but that
truth worked out in relationship: relationship with God,
relationship with one another in the body of Christ, relationships
within the world. It is that truth which liberates us, that truth
which builds us up and that truth which works out in changed
lives. This is our foundation conviction.

It helps us to focus those priorities by asking the question:
'What do I want to leave behind me?' For certainly you will
leave behind you a church at some stage, whether you retire, or
move to another charge. Whatever happens in life, all of us are
in a church, a local congregation, as pastor-teachers, for a limited
period of time. It may be quite a long period of time – some
of us know those who have been in churches forty, fifty years –
or it may be a much shorter period of time. I was told the
other day that the average length of tenure for a Baptist pastor
in some parts of America is eighteen months: long enough for
the first year graphs to come in, and if they are not going up
then you are out. That sort of thinking is not entirely foreign to
the UK in some free church situations. Whether it is insecurity
of tenure or whether it is a long, long ministry, it is in the hand
of God ultimately and his providence. But we can all ask the
question, 'What do I want to leave behind me?' What is your
vision statement? What is your goal for your preaching? I guess

we would perhaps word it in different ways for different congregations, but the biblical concern all the time is for mature disciples who know and love the Lord Jesus and who live the gospel and share the gospel with others. Evangelism and nurture go together. Understanding and relating to God rightly through his word, sharing that word and living that word in the world, these are the great goals that the New Testament encourages us to focus on. We would probably all want to agree to that with different nuances.

The second question I want to ask is, 'How will we get there?' The New Testament would say, 'Teach, teach, teach'. But our problem in the current situation is that we have so little time to do it. It is true that in many churches now Christians are only at church once on a Sunday. Still, thank God, there are people who are there morning and evening, but you have probably noticed (as I have) that evening congregations seem to get smaller and smaller, and that most people make Sunday morning their focus. Now if in Sunday morning's service you have twenty to thirty minutes in which you are teaching the Bible, that is for many of our church members the only input that they have in the week in terms of straightforward teaching of God's truth. I did the maths and found out that that is 0.3 per cent of the week—0.3 per cent sitting under God's word and hearing it taught. It is a minute period of time in the week, particularly when you consider that in the other 99.7 per cent of their week, when they are not sleeping, they are hearing messages that bombard them from a secular culture with all sorts of anti-Christian values. And we think that in twenty to thirty minutes in a week we can actually nurture people, give them strength to fight against the world, the flesh and the devil!

Well, yes, because we believe in the power of the word of God and because we believe in preaching. But it is vital that what we do with that time is of excellent quality, and of course that it does not stand alone, that it is part of a wider strategy to strengthen, build up and equip God's people for works of vice. As we are thinking about the preaching programme, though it is the keystone of the strategy, it does not stand on its own, and we have got to think of all sorts of ways in which the word of God can be set loose in the lives of God's people and those who are not yet his people, as well as the standard preaching in our Sunday services. (Melvin Tinker's chapter gives some helpful suggestions here, especially in the early days of a new ministry.)

Let me suggest five steps that we might take:

1. Assess the current state of the congregation

Take an inventory of where you are at present. Sit down with some of the leaders within the church, along with some other people who are not necessarily in leadership, and talk to them about it. People whose spiritual judgement you respect can help you assess what the current levels of understanding are within the congregation: understanding of the gospel, understanding of the great doctrines of grace, understanding of living the Christian life, understanding of the application of Scripture to life in the world. 'How are we doing as a congregation in our understanding?' Now, you have to do that in an honest way! We shall probably discover that it is much less than we would like it to be and in our more optimistic moments hope it is, because actually levels of understanding across the country are generally low in those areas. Let us be honest about it though, because it begins to open up to us areas of need which our preaching ought to address.

Second, ask what levels of interest and enthusiasm exist for growth in these areas. In other words, as we look at where the levels are currently in the congregation, look for the people who have an appetite to grow. Now again, it would be wonderful if it was 100 per cent, but it will not be. But do go with the people who have an appetite. Feed the people who are hungry, because they will become the feeders of others. Feeding the hungry sheep, in a strategic way in the congregation, is a very important strategy for developing that hunger within the whole flock and lifting the whole level of understanding and relationship with the Lord. Remember that quantity is not necessarily related to quality. There may be people who have a great deal of enthusiasm – but is it being translated into solid understanding of Scripture and a willingness to study the Bible together? I think if I was going to a new church as a pastor for the first time now, what I would look for in the first six months would be two or three people whom I could study the Bible with. I would probably take a little while to choose who they were, and be careful not to make them into a special pastor's elite, but I would look for people who are really hungry to study the Bible. I would work with them on a one-to-one basis following up on what we are doing in the pulpit and in the more formal teaching in other parts of the church's programme. Such people will be a sounding-board to you for your preaching and they will also be able to encourage one another, and you, to work hard at Scripture in trying to increase our own levels of understanding and our own ability to teach it.

Third, ask yourself what is the role of the Sunday preaching in the overall teaching programme? The danger is to say, 'Well, we only have them on Sunday therefore we must give them forty-five minutes.' But this may not be the best way of doing it at all. The fact that they are there and that you want to go for forty-five minutes could be counter-productive. Supposing you inherit a church where they have only ever had a ten minute homily, in which there has been no evangelical ministry over the last few years or in living memory, how would you tackle that? You cannot come in with your thirty to forty minute sermon. Well, you can, but you would probably alienate a lot of people and lose those whom you might win. Some of them will just find it overwhelming at the beginning. I think what you do is that you start to teach them the Bible and you teach them really well for ten minutes or maybe ten and a half the first week, and eleven the second week, and you gradually develop appetite. It is not because you want to get to a magic number, forty, but because you do want to give them as much input as they can take. When Paul says to the Corinthians, 'I couldn't feed you with solid food because you were not yet ready for it' (1 Cor. 3:2), he is rebuking them; they should have been ready. But it is a diagnostic comment. He does not just stuff it into them, whether they are ready for it or not, he goes on feeding them milk until they are ready for it. Where is your congregation? How ready are they? Are they really benefiting from forty-five minutes every Sunday? Is it really going in and being assimilated or would it be better to reduce the amount of material in order to teach more effectively what you do teach? Shorter may be better.

The other way to do this is to have feedback sessions after church to see what people have heard, and what they have remembered. I think it is a very good thing to say (every four to six weeks depending on the length of the series), 'There is an opportunity tonight, after church, for me to answer any questions you have about the sermon series' and be there in an arranged place to take up issues a little bit further. It might last fifteen, thirty, maybe forty-five minutes, depending on interest, on what sort of response you get. Whenever I have done this the really interesting thing is that it has been helpful for me to hear what people have heard me say that I have not said, and what they have not heard that I did say! The feedback from the congregation really helps you to see whether people are learning, whether they are assimilating, or whether they are all sitting there, but not much is happening. So take a realistic inventory about where you are at present and face up to it if you are not cutting much ice.

2. Determine a strategy to help the congregation move forward

Try to establish what would be most helpful. I am picking up Paul's phrase where he says, 'I have not hesitated to preach anything that would be helpful'. I think he is saying that we should not be driven by the congregation's needs, because we shall probably never know all their needs. Only God knows all the needs of our people, but we must do some strategic thinking about what would be most helpful for the church as a congregation at this point in its life. I think there are two ways of doing that: one is the urgent and the other is the long-term. Let me give you a couple of examples because I think this is important in deciding what we are going to preach and how we are going to plan the programme. Out of the inventory exercise (number 1 above), you will probably find that there are certain areas of Christian discipleship, and understanding, which need to be addressed, and therefore you now need to ask yourself, 'What is our strategy for stretching, encouraging and building people up in these areas?' Let us take as a first example evangelism. There are many churches with an impeccable evangelical doctrinal statement who are not evangelistic. Yes, they are thrilled when people come to the Lord, but many people within the church do not have any real strategy or involvement in that. They would say, 'I'm not a gifted evangelist'. So in many evangelical churches the evangelism is at a very low ebb.

If I inherit a congregation like that, and as I recognise it in my inventory, I obviously have to ask myself why. Why is this the situation? Let me suggest there could be a number of reasons. It may be that there is a poor understanding of the gospel. It is a sad fact, but even in 'evangelical' churches, people do not really know what the gospel is. A friend of mine was trying to find a youth worker recently. He advertised, got thirty replies, short-listed eight and asked each of the eight at interview, 'If a teenager said to you, "What's Christianity really all about?", what would be the most important thing to tell them?' Not one of the eight got anywhere near the gospel! So if those young people applying for youth work jobs do not know what the gospel is, you can be fairly sure there are lots of people in the congregation who do not have confidence about what the gospel is. That might need to be a key point in your preaching programme. Or it may be that it is lack of motivation, not just that they do not understand the gospel, but that they are not moved to get the gospel out. Or it may be that they have tried doing it and they have been shot down so that they are now afraid of the non-Christian world. Or it may be that the church has practised isolationism, and holy-huddlism has taken over. They have just kept themselves to themselves, pure and unspotted from the world. All of these could be reasons why the church is not active in evangelism, and all of them need to be addressed through the preaching programme.

So, as you look at what will be most helpful, try to relate how this urgent need would condition the way you think about doing the longer-term preaching programme. If I think there is a poor understanding of the gospel then I would certainly teach the gospel from a Gospel and I would make sure that my preaching programme was focused on that. It is a great place to teach the gospel from; that seems to be why the Gospels were written. It is strange that we often prefer to teach it from the epistles, and that is good, but let us teach the gospel from the Gospels too. Or, if there is a lack of motivation so that the church has become a holy huddle, then teach about the Christian life. Show what it means to live a Christian life in the real world. Breaking down the divisions between the secular and the sacred, which can so easily develop, might be a very powerful sermon series to teach into the deficiencies. Or you might need to build confidence about our identity in Christ. If people are afraid of the non-Christian world, then preach Christ, his victory and power and all that we have in him through his Spirit to build confidence to live godly lives. Or you might look at biblical examples of evangelism: the speeches in Acts, the Lord Jesus encountering different individuals in the Gospels and so on. There are all sorts of ways you could do this, but the preaching programme is not just a matter of saying 'We haven't done Habakkuk for a while, let's do that next'. Usually we need to be much more focused than that if we are going to be really helpful to the congregation. So do this sort of thinking. Where are the areas of immediate need, and what parts of Scripture will address those areas?

Another example: what sort of workers do we need to raise up to reach out with the gospel and grow the church? Why do we not have them already? What is missing? Well, your teaching programme might develop in that direction. Once you have taught what the gospel is, then maybe the need is to have a series in which we teach about the nature of the church, about what it is to be a member of the body of Christ, about holiness and commitment within that context. Or, it could be that something on the ministry of the Holy Spirit is needed. Perhaps there has been such a reaction against excess in that area that nothing has been taught biblically for a long time, and particularly in the area of identifying and using spiritual gifts. There are so many people sitting in our churches unused, who ought to be used, but they are never going to come up and say, 'I'm gifted in this or that'. Most will probably say very humbly, 'I don't have any gifts', so how about teaching them from some of those passages in the New Testament? Or perhaps you will say that the way to do it is to expound Ephesians, and in working through Ephesians all of these issues will be dealt with on the way, which would certainly be true.

None of this is being need-driven. Please notice that; the criteria are not derived from the congregation, they are derived from Scripture and an analysis of the congregation in relation to Scripture. What is the healthy Christian? What is the healthy church? What is the healthy Christian life? It is as we measure our church life against these biblical priorities that we begin to identify areas of need or of help, and to think how best the revelation of Scripture can meet those needs.

3. Work out a balanced diet of teaching

Thirdly, think through the different types of material to be taught. When I was first in the ministry I worked with Leith Samuel, and I remember him saying he was committed to SCEOTS – Systematic Consecutive Exposition Of The Scriptures. I caught this vision from him. That is the way to teach the Bible. So, the first great way of planning a preaching programme is by consecutive biblical exposition. That is the most normal way to do it. There are factors to consider, of course. For example, what balance of biblical material is needed in the next three years or five years? It can be very difficult to think ahead in big chunks of time like that, so the way I would do it would be to look back on the last three years, and see what has been covered. How balanced has it been? Is it a balance of Old Testament, Gospels and epistles? Have we spent more time in one particular area of the Bible than others? (We may do that for very good reason; we need not be obsessed with a perfectly balanced diet according to those rather arbitrary selection and criteria.) But are we actually covering the whole Bible or are there no-go areas that we do not preach on? If we have established that the whole Bible is the whole counsel of God, we need to give a balanced diet over a period of time from the whole of Scripture.

The next question to ask with consecutive exposition is, what length of series? This depends on where you are and the sort of congregation you have. It is going to vary considerably from church to church. I would say that the basic principle is that the series must be long enough to get the melodic line of the book clear so that it is more than just disconnected topics. I sometimes see churches' sermon cards and it is quite fashionable to do Philippians 2 in a month, Isaiah 53 in a month, 1 Peter 1 in a month, Psalm 119 in a month and so on. All you are really getting with that is disconnected bits of the Bible without ever getting the whole meaning, the whole counsel of a particular book clear. One of the things The Proclamation Trust has tried to encourage over the years is thinking about the melodic line: every book has its theme tune. If your series does not get your congregation to the theme tune then they are not going to learn the Bible in the way in which it was written. They are going to learn it cut up into chunks by us, and I do not think we do it as well as God did it! So let us preach the Bible the way God gave us the Bible: book by book.

But you may say that your people cannot take more than a few weeks on a series. That is fine, but then you can do a book over a period of time in a number of mini-series. When I was at Above Bar we preached through John's Gospel in two years on a Sunday evening. Halfway through I asked the congregation if they wanted a break, but they said they wanted to continue. They were a congregation who were trained for that; they valued it and profited from it and I think it was the most effective way of teaching them. But I can imagine another church where if the series was only ever eight or ten weeks, you would need to take John's Gospel and do shorter series, perhaps spread out over a period of three to five years. In that way you still work through and build up their knowledge and their understanding. If we do not do that we shall produce Christians who just know a few favourite verses and a few purple passages but never understand books of the Bible, because the way they are taught from the pulpit is the way they will read the Bible. That is why we want to teach them in the most effective way we can. On balance, I think four weeks for a series is too short. Most churches can cope with at least a ten to twelve week series.

The other consideration in thinking about how to understand the text, work well at it, and prepare the series effectively, is not to try and do it all as a lone ranger. You may be in a church where you are the main preacher, but you still do not have to prepare the sermon series entirely on your own. If there are other people who share the preaching from time to time, particularly if you are in a preaching team, then prepare and study together so that you are agreed on the big picture of the book. If you are sharing the preaching in a series, it is vital that you are not preaching one thing one week, and somebody else contradicting it the next week. Harmony is very important if you are in a preaching team. This is what helps you to see how to divide up the material and how to build a series that really makes sense. Let us suppose we are in a situation where we are at the end of June and thinking now about what we shall preach in September. I would be trying to work now over the next two or three months on what we are going to preach then. Say that in September we are going to preach from Colossians. Well, Dick Lucas has done these wonderful tapes 'From My Study to Yours' – a marvellous resource. But if I roll up in September and listen to the tapes and then write my sermons, what I will find is that by the time I get to the end of the series I am just beginning to understand how to preach Colossians. It would be much better if I understood that before I started the series!

The big fight for us in busy ministries is to have enough time to prepare far enough ahead, not in detail but in preparatory personal study. Over the years I have tried to follow this pattern. When I want to preach new material I make it my personal Bible study material for, say, three months before I come to preach it. Gradually you begin to understand through your own study what the theme lines are, what the major ideas are, how it works. You begin to get it under your belt and feel that you are understanding it now. Then when you come to preach the individual sermon you have got a clearer idea of what the book is about, and if you plan to do this with two or three other people, you can work out how to divide out the material, what is a suitable length and so on.

It may be that you do not have people within the congregation with whom you can do this. But you may be able to join up with some other local ministers in a preaching group. Sharing and discussion of this kind can be very valuable. Do we need to select passages from a long book such as Jeremiah? Or are we going to take Colossians and go through it, and if so at what pace? How many verses a week? I do not mean rigidly, but are we going to do a paragraph a week, a chapter a week? I think the more we can talk that through with others who understand the issues, the better. It may be that you have got to do the basic work, and then come and teach your teaching team so you can think through together how to make this into the most helpful programme for this church at present. Consecutive biblical exposition ought to be the staple diet of the congregation.

Let me make some final comments on the subject of a balanced diet of preaching. Thematic series are good to intersperse between books from time to time. Sometimes you do need to address a particular theme and this is the best way to do it. You might think five or six sermons on prayer are needed, or studies on the pressure of living as a Christian in the contemporary world. Or it may be there is a doctrinal theme you need to deal with: for example, people may need some sermons on Scripture itself and the doctrine of Scripture. These sorts of thematic series are very helpful, provided each of them has a base passage. I think it is very difficult to do systematic lectures on Sunday mornings—they are generally not very profitable for the congregation. But go for a 'home base' passage and teach the doctrine from the passage, perhaps making one or two excursions to cross references. As a variant on the consecutive exposition of books this makes for a good variety within the overall pattern. We are woefully ignorant theologically in church life today. How are we going to teach our people doctrine, good theology? Probably the Sunday morning sermon is not the best place to tackle those things head on. Hopefully there will be good theology throughout your expositions, and they will be learning it as you preach through books. But you might decide that in your preaching programme you want to have a midweek ingredient, where you deal with this from time to time, maybe as a short series. Perhaps you have an annual Bible school when you have a week that is devoted to studying a particular topic, or an occasional Saturday morning seminar or Sunday lunch teach-in. But somehow, somewhere, we have got to be doing a little bit more than just expounding this week's passage if people are really going to get grounded in sound doctrine and sane biblical application. This is secondary to the main diet of the Sunday expository programme, but it is very much needed. The further we can plan ahead on these things, within reason, the better we will do them.

4. Think how to reinforce and complement the Sunday preaching

Think through different contexts of teaching. Ask yourself what are the opportunities to teach, other than in the preaching on Sundays. How can this be reinforced and helped in house-groups for example? Maybe the house-groups can devote themselves to applying what you have taught in the Sunday morning sermon. In Southampton it was always very popular whenever we tied in the house-groups to an application of the Sunday teaching. We always got good feedback about how much more valuable they were. If you try to do exegesis by committee it is almost impossible, and that is what many house-groups are. It is much better for you to teach the passage and let the house-groups discuss the application; this helps take the teaching on to another level. Or maybe Sunday evening, if it is not very well attended, is a time to be used to encourage those who do have appetite to do a different style of study. Somebody I know experimented for a while with preaching through an epistle in the morning and then in the evening taking one verse which had a particular doctrinal or ethical implication and preaching on that in the evening. The Sunday evening congregation started to grow in size because the people who came in the morning, and heard it well taught, wanted to hear something in the evening that took them on to a further stage. Again, we are not just in the business of trying to grow the congregation in size, but in knowledge and love of God, and that was a way of doing it. So be creative, and remember that different people learn differently. We need to plan the series having the congregation in view. I think the danger is that we preach to ourselves, and that our level is the level we pitch it. But do try to think about other people and their levels. Sometimes preachers of my generation forget the younger Christians and do not address sufficiently their needs and concerns. And sometimes preachers of the younger generation forget the older Christians and feel they do not really know what their needs are. Well let me tell you their needs are just the same as the younger Christians! They need to be kept believing, kept faithful, kept focused. But thinking about the groups within the congregation, thinking about how we can relate to them and how the preaching programme is ministering over a period of time to those needs, is well worth doing. It yields great pastoral dividends.

5. Take advantage of opportunities for variety

Use other frameworks to build in variety. If you are in a liturgical based church then the church year provides a certain amount of that in terms of framework, and it may be good to work with that and use it to advantage. Every year those great doctrines of Advent, the Incarnation, the Cross, the Resurrection and Pentecost provide some shape, and those of us who are not in such a framework could sometimes make an excursion into it.

Pastoral needs can help guide us. There are people in our congregations who are discouraged and drifting, so maybe it would be good to have a short series on the dangers of drift. Use Hebrews for example, to analyse the reasons why we drift, and what the Bible teaches us about our hearts as a result of that, and what remedies it sets in place. There are certainly people in our congregation who are what I would describe as rooted but rutted. That is a pastoral need that needs to be addressed; you cannot just let them go on. It is a sad thing when there are people in their sixties who have learnt nothing since their twenties. Those are people I am concerned about. So how do I get under their radar screen in my preaching to get through their defences? Is my series addressing some of those needs as well as building up the new Christians who are exciting and excited and who are a great joy to be with? And then there are always the resistant, the rebellious, the people with low expectations. So think about the framework of pastoral needs when you plan your programme.

Then of course there are the special events. I think they are best kept to a few but it is good to have a missions weekend, maybe a Tear Fund Sunday; lots of churches have a Church Birthday Sunday and other special guest services. You can overdo it – I grew up in a context where it was quite common for churches to have all sorts of anniversaries, but it meant that they were always breaking up the teaching programme. It is better to reduce them to a smallish number and do them well, but to keep on teaching the word on that consecutive basis through your series.

GETTING DOWN TO THE TASK

Assessing the state and needs of our congregation, determining a forward-moving strategy, planning a balanced diet of Sunday teaching, reinforcing this in a variety of other ways and taking advantage of every opportunity that offers itself to us – it all sounds very daunting! But remember that it is God himself, through the word of his grace, who does the real work. This is our great assurance, and it is this confidence – that God is at work – that enables us to knuckle down to the task in hand, the hard work of sustaining the preaching and teaching programme we have set before ourselves. In the next chapter we shall consider some of the practicalities involved in carrying out this task as it confronts us week by week.

3
From Text to Sermon

David Jackman

Imagine the scene. People are coming out of church on Sunday morning, and you have preached your heart out in the morning service. Various people have been looking after the kids in the crèche or teaching Sunday school, and one of them meets someone who has been in the main meeting and says, 'Did you have a good time in church this morning?' 'Yes, we had a really good time.' 'So what was the sermon about?' Now at this point is the moment of truth. Can that person tell us what the sermon was about in the soundbite that a conversation on the church path requires? Often, alas, the answer is a little less clear than we would like it to be!

Preaching with clarity and preaching with relevance is a demanding goal for all of us as expositors of the Bible. It is a goal we often fall short of, but one that we continually need to make our aim. Jim Packer says in one of his essays, that many sermons suffer from 'muddle in the middle'. Sadly, far too many sermons fall into John Stott's categories when he says in many churches there are only three types of sermons: the dull, the duller and the inconceivably dull. So it is not surprising that people say, 'What is to be done about preaching?' If we as preachers stop asking that question we are very soon going to be in the inconceivably dull category. But in practice many of us place preaching well down the list of ministry priorities. We do not actually ditch it – it has got to be done – but it is not very high on many people's list of priorities. Methodologically it is under fire. It is overtly and excessively didactic, which does not fit with our culture. It is non-participatory and it lacks the visual stimulus that you need for 'effective contemporary communication'. I was told recently that the average concentration span of someone at the beginning of listening is now seven seconds, and asked how you get them hooked in seven seconds? Well, I think if it is only seven seconds, I am a non-combatant! I do not think you can get people hooked in seven seconds, but there is that little moment at the beginning when you either start to fly or you are facing difficulties! So in the return on time investment, many a busy minister has decided, even if subconsciously, to cut preparation time to the minimum and to devote his energies and interest to activities which seem to yield better and more immediate results. That is why many ministers are so bogged down with administration, with pastoral visits and counselling sessions that when they come to address the congregation all they have is a devotional soundbite, perhaps stretched out to fill the allotted fifteen, twenty or maybe thirty minutes. The view is clearly that these alternative priorities will actually produce a more active and positive church than spending hours in preparing the sermon.

The pew controlling the pulpit

It is an amazing paradox that now, when we have more aids to teaching the Bible and more opportunity to understand Christian truth than ever before, we are arguably one of the most biblically ignorant generations for centuries. Everywhere, in the church as well as outside, there is a dearth of biblical understanding, because there is an absence of clear biblical applied teaching. There is a line in one of Milton's poems in which he says, 'The hungry sheep look up and are not fed'. He could be writing about the church in Britain today. The appetites of many starving Christians are not being satisfied.

We need to ask ourselves why, because many of us begin ministries saying, 'Oh yes, I'm going to be a preacher. I'm going to devote myself to preaching.' But somewhere along the line we lose the impetus and the focus. In Eugene Petersen's stimulating book, *Working the Angles*, he suggests that one of the reasons why we have problems is that we are all customers and consumers now, and many of our churches are run as though they are spiritual supermarkets. People come in and they want to be pleased with the service they receive. They really come to purchase the commodities and the brands they think they need. So we respond to that by encouraging and rewarding loyalty and we have our own brands of loyalty cards and loyalty points for people who keep turning up. The preachers know that they need to find something useful for people's lives and to benefit their hearers, and also to meet their expectations of them as Christian professionals who can deliver the goods. So, says Petersen, the result is that, just as in so many areas of contemporary culture, in the church too we have become the prisoners of our own marketing. The pew is controlling the pulpit.

'Bible-based' ministry is not biblical ministry

What does that look like in terms of preaching? It means that we start to plunder the Bible to get what we want out of it. The text has to be startling: it has to be an arresting text, if possible a dramatic text. The passage has to provide the right psychological feel-good effect, and the proof-text must underline the framework of our particular theological camp. What Petersen is saying is that we are falling into the trap of looking at the Bible rather than listening to the Bible. There is a subtle difference we must note here. We have shifted from being governed by Scripture in the contents and methods of ministry, to regarding the Bible as a possession over which we have control, a source book that can act as a springboard for our own more 'relevant' approach. In the end, what has happened in the church is that we have started to domesticate God's word, we have tamed it to suit our pulpit purposes. Evangelicals often talk about having a Bible based ministry, but from that base they can safely travel over the hills and far away! What we should be concerned for is a thoroughly biblical ministry, seeking for ourselves and for our churches to have what was memorably said of John Bunyan – that he had bibline blood.

In order to remedy this situation, preachers need to maintain confidence in the word of God that is preached, and in the preaching of the word of God. We need to regain certain inescapable biblical priorities, not just as an intellectual position, but as the bloodstream of our ministry. Central to the whole ethos of New Testament Christianity is the need to receive and to pass on to others the unchanging and revealed truth of Almighty God. The Bible is God preaching to us about God, and we need to take seriously that divine purpose in giving us this incredible treasure, the infallible revelation of sixty-six books of canonical Scripture. It is typical of the arrogance of our culture to imagine that we have outgrown the need for such written revelation. In big evangelical jamborees now, in talk after talk, a Bible verse is read out at the beginning, the Bible is symbolically shut and we go off on something else. It is so easy for people to assume that is what the Bible is: just the springboard, just an occasional focus. All the time we fail to realise the truth: that the time has come when men will not put up with sound doctrine, and instead are gathering around them a great number of teachers to say what their itching ears want to hear (2 Tim. 4:3).

Making the word of God fully known

One of the clearest reflective summaries of all this is Paul's great aim for his own ministry stated at the end of Colossians 1. He says in verse 25: 'I became a minister according to the stewardship from God which was given to me for you, to make the word of God fully known.' That is the great calling – both of the apostle and of everyone who stands in the apostolic succession – that we are called to make the word of God fully known. That is the stewardship from God, given to us for the church. He tells us that this word of God is fully revealed in the Lord Jesus, the mystery hidden for ages and generations, but now revealed to his saints, and that 'the glorious riches of this mystery' is 'Christ in you, the hope of glory' (v.27). So when we talk about preaching Christ we mean teaching the whole counsel of God, the word of God in all its fullness because Christ is the centre of all the Scriptures. And as we preach Christ, as we proclaim him, the effect of that ministry of the whole word of God is that we understand Christ in us now, and the hope of glory in the future. We are rooted both in the present and the future, and both of these perspectives are essential in a biblical teaching ministry.

The very familiar verses of Colossians 1:28-29 are important:

> We proclaim him, admonishing and teaching
> everyone with all wisdom, so that we may
> present everyone perfect in Christ. To this end
> I labour, struggling with all his energy, which
> so powerfully works in me.

But in chapter 2 Paul goes on to say 'I want you to know how much I am struggling for you and for those at Laodicea, and for all who have not met me personally'. How does he struggle for the Colossians he has not seen? He does so in writing this letter and, as the letter tells us, by constantly praying for them.

When we see what he is writing this letter to achieve, we come again into a focus on preaching, for Colossians 2:2-4 show us the congregational outworking of making the word of God fully known. We so often individualise it, but Paul is writing to a whole church. And the sort of church that he longs for the preaching of the word to produce is one where believers' hearts are encouraged, knit together in love, and reaping all the riches of full assurance of understanding and the knowledge of God's mystery – which is Christ, in whom are hidden all the treasures of wisdom and knowledge.

First, Paul wants the Colossian church to be encouraged in heart. The idea here is Christ himself, the Christ who is in them, strengthening them through his word, encouraging, putting courage into them as a congregation. He wants them to be united in love – 'knit together in love' – and he wants them to be reaching all the riches of full assurance of understanding, so that no-one may delude them with plausible arguments. So, encouragement comes through the ministry of the word, and this in turn brings the church together in the reality of Christian love and deepens understanding of the full knowledge of Christ (who is the source of all wisdom and knowledge). This is what makes the church resistant to clever plausible impressive arguments, either from false teachers within the church or from the culture outside the church.

This is comprehensive: an encouraged congregation united in love, with a complete understanding of the full knowledge of the Lord Jesus so that whatever pressures are on them from inside or outside they are immune to cultural deception. All this is achieved through this ministry of the word that Paul has talked about in chapter 1. He is effecting this ministry as he writes the letter and as he prays for the congregation, just as he is doing it in the congregations that he sees face to face. But even though the Colossians do not see him, that is still Paul's ministry to them and for them. In other words, whatever the situation, he is not content to be merely 'Bible-based'; he determines to make the word of God fully known. This is the pattern of ministry which we also are to engage in. So how do we do it today?

FROM TEXT TO SERMON

One of the particular challenges for us concerns the peculiarity of our contemporary context. I think this is what often unnerves us as preachers today. Obviously we cannot afford to be blind to our culture. We have to build bridges into people's minds and hearts if God's Son and God's truth are to be conveyed to them through our preaching. But the bridges of yesterday cannot accomplish that task today; glorious though those bridges often were they do not actually make connection with the contemporary world. So, I want to suggest ten pieces of advice by which our preaching might be helped to become clearer, more relevant and effective as we think about doing this job in our culture.

1. Get rid of the idea that we have to make the text relevant

We often lose confidence because the fundamental conviction, that when the Bible is properly explained and understood then God's voice is heard with power today, is quite hard to hold onto in practice. It is a challenge to go on really believing it: that God himself is the teacher, instructing his people about his character and his purposes, that he is the one who illuminates our understanding about ourselves and about our world. Yet unless the Bible is being taught that way, as indeed it presents itself, of course the church is not going to be able to cope with living in contemporary culture. However, if we believe that every part of the Bible is God preaching God to us, in a variety of genres and in many different presentations, we can have confidence that what he has inspired and preserved as a living word, is the word to us now, as much as it was to every preceding generation.

An invasive message from God

But the teacher is also the invader. CS Lewis has a memorable phrase when he calls God 'the transcendental interferer', and as soon as you open up the Bible, you begin to find God doing that in your life. He communicates his truth to us because he loves us, and for that same reason he invades our sin-blinded minds and hardened hearts and consciences, in order to change us. This is what preaching does. This is what preaching is all about; it is not just simply laying out the truth of the message, but it is in the invasion of the living God through his word into the mind, heart and will of the hearer. It is very unsettling, very challenging, and very demanding. John Stott expresses this memorably when he speaks about the purpose of preaching being 'to disturb the comfortable and then to comfort the disturbed'. Does our preaching do both of those things? When we are preaching are we disturbing the comfortable? I do not mean going out and gripping the congregation by the jugular and making life exceedingly unpleasant for people. There is a certain sort of 'beating up' style of preaching, where you can go to church and get hit over the head every week! I do not mean that. But are we allowing the word of God to speak in all its fullness so that our comfort levels really are disturbed? That will happen in the study first, before it ever happens in the pulpit. Then comes also the healing balm of God's word, as it truly comforts the disturbed when we turn to him in repentance, in renewed faith or in renewed obedience, or whatever it may be.

It is this total confidence that the word of God will do the work of God which is the basis of our preaching ministry. There are many famous comments about it. Luther said 'I just threw the Bible into the congregation and the word did the work', and that is right. It is the word that does the work; that is why I spend so much time preparing it, because I do believe that the word of God through the power of the Spirit of God does the work of God. It is not my job, therefore, to have to find some way to make it relevant. My job is to teach this biblical text properly within its own context and to do so in order that the word is set free so that it makes its own impact. This is the way the invading God, through his Spirit, reaches into the minds and hearts of the hearers.

Exposition not journalism

Now we find this quite hard. Many of us are tempted away to what I call journalistic preaching rather than expository preaching, because of our culture. Because we live in the soundbite culture we face this contemporary challenge, but the way in which we often meet it is to accept the values of the culture and to copy its methodology, and this is what leads us into journalistic preaching. Just what is this 'journalistic preaching'? A couple of characteristics, comparing journalistic preaching with expository preaching, will help us see. Journalistic preaching says: 'I have got to do something with the Bible. I have got to construct a sermon, I have got to do something with the Bible so there is something to give on Sunday.' Expository preaching says: 'The Bible has got to do something with me.' The Bible is setting the agenda in expository preaching, whereas I am setting the agenda in journalistic preaching. Journalistic preaching is interested in the issues of the moment, in other words it follows the world's agenda. I am not saying we should be deaf to that agenda but we must not let it dictate our preaching. Expository preaching is interested not in the issues of the moment, but in the issues of eternity; it is interested in God's agenda, rather than the particular cultural agenda we happen to live in.

Journalistic preaching therefore is interested in being witty and amusing. It is strong on stories and clever illustration, whereas expository preaching is interested in being powerful and penetrating in the spiritual sense of the truth changing people's lives. Of course good expository preaching will have good illustrations and it may well be amusing and witty also. But ask where the focus is in the preaching. It is very tempting to think that one has to start off with a joke or two. I remember one of our African students at The Proclamation Trust's Cornhill Training Course telling me he could never be an English preacher because he would never know which jokes to tell at the beginning! That was what he had picked up about English preaching. Why? Because it has become a sort of cultural thing that you have to do that at the start of a sermon. It is like journalism, you have got to have an attention grabber, a funny remark or something outrageous to say. Now, of course you do want to gain people's attention. But what is the motivation? Journalistic preaching is preacher focused, so you come out saying, 'what a great communicator'. Expository preaching is Christ focused, so that you come out saying, 'What a great and gracious Saviour'. Journalistic preaching is ephemeral because it will be used tomorrow to wrap up the fish and chips; that is what journalism is. Expository preaching is life shaping, it is preparing people for heaven.

Think about your recent sermons. How journalistic have they been and how expository are they? How much confidence do you really have that the word of God will do the work? This is not an excuse for being boring or dull. But let us get rid of the idea that we have got to make the Bible relevant, that we have got to put on a performance. No, we have to be faithful and clear, and if we do that people will be enormously helped. The main aim of the sermon is not for them to know how clever we are, but to know what a great God we serve and what a wonderful Saviour Jesus is, and that Christ is in us, the hope of glory.

2. Do the hard work on what the text means

All effective biblical proclamation depends on good quality exegesis of the text, and there are no short cuts to that. It is not just the exploration of vocabulary, word studies, or the structure of the argument or the narrative, but the understanding of the meaning of the text in its original context. We do have to travel back in time to the situation in eighth-century Jerusalem BC as indicated within the biblical book itself if we are to take Isaiah's message and bring it to the twenty-first century. If we do not see why Paul wrote what he wrote to Corinth, we shall never be able to preach its message in London or New York or anywhere else. This is a basic principle which we preachers have heard many, many times. But are we doing it? Are we really giving a good chunk of our study time to getting the meaning right? If not, we will obviously not get it right in terms of what it means for us today.

We all know the enormous help it is when through preaching, a light is switched on and we are suddenly brought to see the meaning of a text with clarity so that we say, 'Oh, now I see it. How stupid of me not to see it there before!' That is the great blessing that so often comes through preaching: you hear God's word in a fresh way. But that only comes if you have worked hard at the text and tried to sort out that meaning with some discipline. Then, when you are preaching, what you are doing is explaining – expounding – the meaning. We often express this under three headings – state, explain, apply, and of the three our greatest weakness is usually in the explaining. We are not bad at stating main points. Application is hard but we have a good attempt at it. But the missing link often is explaining. How much of your sermon is taken up actually explaining the meaning of the text? When we preach the Bible like that, then we preach with biblical authority. Conversely, if we do not explain the Scripture and then apply what the passage says, then we actually undermine the Bible's authority and we invest authority in ourselves and our sermon, rather than in God and his word. If that happens ultimately people come to believe that anything with a biblical flavour is what God is saying. Haddon Robinson points out that the long-term effect of this is that we preach mythology – an element of truth, along with a great deal of puff. And the problem is that 'people tend to live in the puff. We live in the implication of implications and then they discover that what they thought God promised he didn't promise at all.'

Now is that not true of a lot of so-called 'teaching'? It has some of biblical flavour – it sounds vaguely biblical – but because the preacher has not worked on the text, there is no conviction that this is the real meaning of this passage of Scripture. There is no driving it home in terms of understanding, so you are left merely with general implications and all sorts of 'Well it might be this or it might be that'. If we are to avoid this, we must do the hard work on what the text means.

3. Make sure the original context determines your contemporary application

Application is very stretching for all of us but the greatest help I find in application is to understand why the Bible writer addressed this issue with these people in this text and why he expressed it in this way, in these words. Once I have understood why this text is here in its own context, then from this original context the contemporary application begins to be suggested. It is largely a matter of drawing the correct lines of continuity from the biblical text to the contemporary congregation. When we start off at Cornhill each year doing sermon classes, most people know that it is a good idea to apply the biblical text. So all good Proclamation Trust students in the first term bring an invisible bag which is marked 'Bolt-on applications evangelical preachers can use', and these bolt-on applications flow freely in the first term! This is very understandable, because that is the way they have heard it done. There are several bolt-on applications, and there are certain things a preacher can always say. We can say that we ought to read the Bible more, we ought to pray more, we ought to witness more. All these things are perfectly correct, but if you get that all the time you soon learn how to defend your wicket against it; you soon know that is the switch-off point. We have got to make application which (to change the metaphor) goes under the radar screen, and the only way to get that sort of application is to work so hard on why the Bible says it here and in this way, that it illuminates your understanding about what it means to us today in our context.

God then and God now

Let us examine some of those connecting lines. The strongest line of application is from God then to God now. What God said then, who God was then, how God acted then, is exactly the same as what God says, is and does now. So you know that anything the passage is teaching you about God is going to be true now because of his unchanging eternal nature. This is a very obvious point, but are you teaching the character of God as you apply the Bible – that the God of then is the God of now? There will also often be links, in Old Testament passages, between Israel as his covenant people and the church as his new covenant people; and many clear applications flow from this. In making the continuity link it is also important to recognise, of course, the discontinuity: we are not in exactly the same position as the Old Testament covenant community was. The work of Christ on the cross has happened and the fruit of Christ's triumph, the gift of the Spirit, has been poured out to indwell the believer. The new covenant promises of Jeremiah and Ezekiel have been fulfilled in the gospel for us. We are therefore in a different relationship and not just the equivalent of the church in the desert.

But there are many links from covenant people in the old

covenant to people in the new, because it is the same God dealing on the same principles with his people. Similarly, the Old Testament passages which speak to the nations of the world will have direct application to the sinful rebellious world all around us, and to our nation. We shall also need to recognise that the specific terms of the issue at stake may have changed, so that we do not simply pick up from the Old Testament a wooden literalism. Rather, we need to read the Old Testament from the basis of the new in the light of the fuller revelation; as JI Packer puts it, reading the Bible backwards as well as forwards. But the original context will always help you in contemporary application.

Let us consider a New Testament example. In the letter to the Galatians the presenting issues are the Judaisers and their insistence on food laws, circumcision and so on. Now, these are hardly current issues in any church in Britain today. Therefore it is very easy to wonder how Galatians relates today. We will have to go the historical route, teach the history, and show what was happening and why it was happening. But when we establish the context, and really study the letter to the Galatians, we find that the Judaisers were using circumcision and food laws as the entrance requirement to a sort of super spiritual club, to an elite. What they were saying was in effect, 'Of course you have salvation through faith in Jesus, but if you want to be really spiritual Christians, then you must add to your basic faith these Jewish things as well.' And Paul's argument, in broad terms, is that by adding to the gospel they are in fact destroying the gospel; trying to get people into their elite group will actually be bondage not freedom, but it is for freedom Christ has set you free.

Once you see that in the larger context of Galatians, the contemporary parallels in the early twenty-first century are legion – they stand up and wave at you! It is not simply about circumcision and the food laws, but about the way in which we may make many things, which are good and right in themselves, an addition to the gospel of Christ. The church today is awash with 'gospel-plus' groups who want to claim a superior spirituality on the grounds of their particular emphasis or their particular experience. It is by working at the context that you begin to see how, though the packaging changes from century to century, the same issue, the same basic challenge, is still here today as it was in first century Galatia. And now the whole book starts to become alive in a new way to the contemporary congregation. So make sure the original context determines your contemporary application.

4. Set the passage in its wider biblical and theological context

This is very basic. We often set the passage in its book context, and see that what has gone before and what comes after illuminates our understanding. But set each passage in the whole Bible context as well. Ask yourself how this finds its place in the whole biblical revelation. On this basis we are comparing Scripture with Scripture, believing it to be a unity and a revealed whole. We are allowing Scripture to be self-interpreting in dependence on the Holy Spirit's illumination, so we must pray that we may see how this passage works in the great spread of Scripture, in the big picture of salvation history. We need to draw on our understanding of biblical theology. What does this text uniquely teach us about the gracious purposes of God between creation and the new creation? How does it sing in tune with that great sweep of the salvation history plan of God? If Christ is the centre and theme of all the Scriptures (as the Bible clearly says he is) then how does this point to the Lord Jesus? How can I preach Christ from this passage?

We must also turn to the discipline of our systematic theology to the big picture of a completed revelation about God and the world, to enable us to relate what this particular passage is teaching doctrinally to the wider flow and the richer perspective of the whole Bible. If we do not reflect on that, we will end up preaching parts of the Bible in an unbalanced way without the checks and balances of thinking about how this passage fits into the whole. That can very quickly erode our confidence, and our hearers' confidence, because over a period of time it seems as though we are preaching contradictory doctrines. Do not misunderstand me. I am not saying that sermons should serve up slabs of biblical or systematic theology. But I am saying that the preacher must reflect on both and then decide how much needs to be included in the sermon, so that the truths of a particular text are rightly related to the teaching of Scripture as a whole.

Preaching New Testament grace

The importance of this theological reflection can be illustrated by seeing how we so easily turn grace into law. It is so natural for us to go back to works religion, and unless careful about it, evangelicals often preach the grace of God as law: a whole new set of instructions that we ought to keep. If, for example, you are going to preach your way through the Sermon on the Mount, you start with the Beatitudes of course. You talk about how important it is to recognise that entry into the kingdom is only to the spiritually bankrupt who mourn for their sins, only to those who humble themselves, who hunger and thirst for righteousness. That is the way in – all by grace – and that is what the sermon is teaching us. But then when we get on to Jesus saying 'Unless your righteousness exceeds that of the Pharisees …' we start to think, 'Well how can it?' It must be by keeping all these rules. So we forget the Beatitudes and we go straight on to make it all law, as though it was not about grace at all! We say 'Well of course we fail all the time to do that', and so the sermon is here to teach us, as Luther said, 'to crawl to Christ'. But, what happens when you crawl to Christ? Does he not say to you: 'My grace is sufficient for you. My grace has met your need.' That is why this kingdom is open to the spiritual bankrupts and the mourners and the meek and the hungry – because of God's grace to us in Christ! And yes, he sends us back to live according to the instruction he gives, but not as the fruit of legalism and law-keeping, rather as the response to the grace that has reached us in the gospel. The New Testament is a gospel of grace, and we must preach it as grace.

Preaching Old Testament grace

But so is the Old Testament a gospel of grace! Why did God give the law in Exodus 19-23? Because he had already redeemed a people whom he wants to show the way to live in order to please him. How then, as God's covenant people, do you enjoy covenant blessings? By keeping the covenant obligations. But it is not keeping the covenant obligations that puts you into the covenant. It is grace that puts you into the covenant and you live in the covenant through the obedience that comes by grace, through faith. What is true in Exodus is true in Matthew. Unless you balance things like that, unless you think about the wider biblical and theological context, you will very easily slip into legalism. I was preaching in an impeccable evangelical church recently, and they had a children's talk in the morning which was taken from one of the children's picture books, which told us very clearly with lovely pictures how God rescued Noah because he was a righteous man. Apparently, God is working in Genesis on the basis of works religion; you are saved by your works in Genesis! So the children all grow up thinking the Old Testament is different from the New Testament: works in the Old Testament and grace in the New Testament. It so quickly slips in. Now that church would have been horrified if someone had told them that was what they were teaching, but it just crept in through the lady who was giving the children's talk because the book said it, and they were nice pictures – and so we were all taught that Noah was saved because he was a righteous man.[2] But if you read Genesis, what does it say? 'Noah found grace in

---

[2] It is amazing how many children's Bibles and story books are guilty of this. We need to be alert that we are not drumming works religion into our kids unawares.

the eyes of the Lord'. And this is what came out of it: Noah was a righteous man. As Alec Motyer puts it, grace found Noah first and made him righteous. It is that sort of theological balance that we must keep thinking about. Expository preaching also must be theologically balanced preaching.

5. Focus your understanding and purpose in key sentences

It is a great discipline in preparing the sermon to have a theme sentence and an aim sentence. The theme sentence sums up the big idea of the passage; it is what you must teach from this passage. It is having the theme sentence right that delivers you from muddle in the middle. If you have not got a clear theme sentence in your mind you will probably have several sermons shaken up together in a bag, each of them desperately trying to escape from one another, and there will not be any cohesion in what you do. So when you have done the basic work on the text and reflected on its context, and therefore its application, set it in the wider biblical theological context. Try to focus on exactly what is the big idea of this particular passage. What is the message (an old-fashioned word, but a good word) that I must preach from this text? We are back to our question on the church path – 'what was the sermon about?' Does your sermon have a message that is clearly taught? If you as the preacher does not know what it is, then the congregation does not stand a chance. It is part of our love for the congregation to work hard at a theme sentence that is clear and focused, that says, 'This is the message'.

Tied to the theme sentence is the aim sentence. This is what you are praying the Holy Spirit will be pleased to do in the lives of the hearers as a result of this sermon. After all if there is no clear aim, why bother? Once the sentences are formulated in your mind, allow them to discipline the whole preparation process. This is a tremendous help against that tempting excursion away from the main road, into by-path meadow with its delusive digressions, which confuse people because they are really nothing to do with the main theme. Focus your understanding in the theme sentence, and your purpose in the aim sentence, and pray your purpose through all the time you are writing up your notes. All the time you are structuring your sermon, make that aim your prayer: 'Lord, this is the purpose of the passage, please work it out in people's lives like this.' God may well do all sorts of other things through it, but we have a responsibility to have a clear aim that we are praying through, and that aim must flow from the clear exposition of the passage before us.

6. Develop a clear and coherent presentation

The magical mystery tour is not a good paradigm for preaching, so it is important and worthwhile to try and express the major ideas in clear points and work hard to show their interdependence. It may seem very obvious, but quite often I listen to sermons where the points are not really very clear at all. They are probably there, lurking under the surface, but there is a great value and real help to your hearers in highlighting your main points. There do not have to be three points; the text will show you how many there are, and it is perfectly possible to preach a sermon with one main point, or with two. If it is five, then you possibly have too long a passage! Don't be suffocated, but do try to put your message into a number of main points. It is very helpful if those main points convey, as they are stated, the main teaching of the message. In other words, make your headings didactic points rather than descriptive points. For example, if your heading is simply 'The Faith of Abraham', that tells you very little. But if you say 'People who believe God do something' (whatever Abraham is doing in the story), then you have a didactic point that takes the reference away from Abraham exclusively in the past and relates it to the present. It also takes it out of the particularity of Abraham and translates the point into the particularity of the congregation, and so underlines the unchanging principle being taught.

Main points are like marker-posts and are tremendously important; they aid the memory of the hearer and give structure. They also give pace and balance to the construction of the sermon because if you know you have four main points to make, and you only have twenty minutes to preach, you can time things properly. It is no good taking eight minutes on each point! People think that by some amazing miracle fifteen minutes' worth of material can be compressed into five minutes when you stand up and give it, but of course it won't! It will expand rather than contract, so if you know you only have twenty-five minutes (or whatever it is) to preach, work out how long you are going to spend on each point. Is it an important or subsidiary point? Do not spend three or four minutes on an illustration that is not germane to the main thrust of the sermon. The more you think like that about structure, the clearer your sermon will be. One of the things I always pray for is clarity; people need to hear the word of God plainly. Our problem is that we usually have too many ideas by the time we have done all the exegetical work. Our notes are full of all sorts of 'children' that have been given birth to in this process, who are clamouring to be put in the sermon! But some of these children have to be sacrificed because they do not fit in with the main message of the sermon. Only when you have started to think like this will you achieve clarity. If you are undisciplined about it then you will just waffle.

7. Study your congregation

It was said of the Puritans that they spent as much as half of their time in preaching on the application, and certainly, if you read their sermons, there is a very deep pastoral concern and acute awareness of the condition of their hearers in all the variety of life. It is not a bad thing to think about your congregation in various categories. In terms of where they are in spiritual experience, for example, are there unconverted people there? Are there new Christians? Are there old Christians who have stopped growing? Are there discouraged Christians? Think about them in terms of what you know through your pastoral care of them so that your preaching is related to the reality. Or you could think about them in terms of the spheres of life in which they work: their home lives, their work lives, the community life, the personal thought life of all of us as individuals. These are areas in which application can be focused and applied, so that the lens can be sharpened a little more.

When we are thinking about application to the whole congregation, the focus evident in Colossians 2 is surely important. We want the application to be producing a congregation encouraged in their faith, united in their love, able to appreciate the fullness of the riches of the gospel and increasingly immune to the pressures of the culture which will drive them away from that gospel. How is your preaching going to help them to do that? What is there in Sunday sermons that meets any of those things? I am not saying that in every sermon you do all of it, of course. But these are good grids to operate to ensure that we are working biblically and working practically for greater focus and greater clarity in what we do. The better we know the congregation the more we should be able to do it.

8. Apply the truth to the whole person

Martyn Lloyd-Jones said that the purpose of the preacher is to take God's truth through the mind, to the heart, to activate the will. That is a brilliant definition of what is going on in preaching. What is there in your Sunday sermon for the mind? How does this sermon help people to understand God's truth? How does it expose false ideas? How does it expose evil and how does it convince the mind of the truth of what this passage is saying? That is why Paul reasoned, argued and explained. The heart, here, is not so much the centre of the emotions as we tend to think of it. In the Bible the heart is the control centre of the personality where you make your decisions, where you decide on the direction of your life. So, the question we must ask is whether we are taking the truth from the mental cognition of what it means, to an application to the control centre of the lives of the people. Do I show them the miseries of sin or do I just talk about sin? Do I show them the joys of obedience, the blessings of the gospel, the challenges of obedience and commitment? It is more than just truth for the mind; it is the heart being impacted by the way in which the word is taught, so that the hearer says, 'I do want to go there. I do want to be like that. I do want to grow in my knowledge and love of Jesus.'

Thirdly, does it activate the will? Do we move beyond 'Oh that was a lovely sermon, wasn't it great?' to 'How am I going to obey it this week?' The will has to be activated, the promises have to be believed, sin has to be repented of, remedies have to be appropriated, faith has to be exercised. If you have none of those ingredients (mind, heart, will) you are not preaching to the whole person. Martin Allen has more to say on this in the next chapter; it is a matter of vital importance.

9. Make your language count

We live in a culture where for many people language does not count, because often our language is so flattened out and feeble. But preachers do need to be wordsmiths. This does not mean complicated vocabulary; it means being skilled in employing the variety and diversity of our language to be able to enrich people's thought and understanding through carefully chosen words. The English language is greatly abused these days. Much spoken English is flat, cliché ridden and imprecise. I read recently that the problem today is that any noun can be 'verbed'! So, we need to use language intelligently and thoughtfully, and when we do, it is a help to people. I am not asking that you become a rhetorician; but can you paint a picture in words? Do you practise painting vivid pictures? When you illustrate can people see what you are illustrating? Do you use metaphors and similes in a way that arrests attention and tries to identify what you mean with pinprick accuracy, so that it is really clear? Or are you one of those preachers who go in for abstractions and generalisations? So many sermons are loaded with phrases like 'We ought to be better witnesses at home and in the workplace' or, worse, 'I must leave you to work this one out, time forbids me to deal with it here…' This approach is so flattening and disappointing because the words are vague and general and the ideas are not developed to any effect. Little wonder if people do not respond—they do not respond because it is inconceivably dull!

Try to make your language as alive, as vivid, as real as you can. That means thinking carefully about it. Whether you write it all down and preach from a script, or whether you prefer to think it through and try to remember how to say it in the pulpit using only notes, at some stage you do need to think clearly how you are going to say it. The only person responsible for the words up there is you, so make your language count.

10. Pray for the Holy Spirit to blow his life-giving breath through it all

Finally, it is vitally important in all of this that we are not just simply writing an essay for people to read. We are not just concocting a 'talk' which we hope will engage them. We are concerned with the work of preaching the living word of God; there is no task that is more privileged, and no task that is more responsible. Therefore we desperately need the Holy Spirit to illuminate us in our understanding and then, in the preaching of the God-given word, to blow his life-giving breath through it all, and to do the gracious and powerful work that only he can do.

How much we really are men of faith is marked by how

much we actually pray for this – for the work of the Spirit of God in the preaching. I find it far easier to spend much, much more time on my preparation than on my prayer, and yet I know that this impoverishes the preaching. We need to repent of this, because the inspirer of the Bible is also the illuminator of the Bible's readers and the Bible's hearers, and the empowerer of the Bible's preachers. If preaching is going to happen – not just lecturing, but preaching by which people's lives are changed – then we are totally dependent on the Spirit's working. The whole process of preparation must therefore be prayed through and carried out in conscious dependence on God. In some ways it is great when we are stuck on a sermon because it makes us pray more! When it is really tough, and all too often only then, we do cry out to the Lord, and I think I have learned that that is part of God's gracious care of us that he makes us dependent on him in that way. The congregation, too, has a vital responsibility to pray for the preacher, and for the preaching. Only this sort of preaching – prayer saturated preaching – will bring the breath of life to those who hear it.

The answer to the present crisis is not less preaching but better preaching. That is a challenge to every preacher, every time we preach. To his students, two or three generations ago, it is said that W Griffith Thomas put it this way:

> Think yourself empty, read yourself full,
> write yourself clear, pray yourself keen,
> then into the pulpit and let yourself go!

Put the clutter away and concentrate on God. Read yourself full in the word and in all the things that help you understand the word. Write yourself clear, because you do not really know you have understood it until you have written it down clearly. Pray yourself keen, and then into the pulpit and be yourself – let yourself go! We can trust God to do what only he can do if we have committed ourselves to the task like that.

4

Preaching to Real People

Martin Allen

There is not much written on the people to whom we preach. Plenty has been written on the preacher and his message, the preacher and his God, the preacher and himself even—but not much on the preacher and the people. We find little more than a single chapter in preaching textbooks headed 'Pastoral Preaching' or 'The Congregation'. Yet it is a vital subject, perhaps more so today than ever before, with the massive turning away from church and preaching. In his book *I Believe in Preaching,* John Stott cites a nineteenth-century author, Austin Phelps, who said that a thoroughly trained preacher is first a human being, at home among human beings, and then a scholar, at home in libraries. And, Stott adds, 'I am glad that the emphasis begins with people not books. The best preachers are always diligent pastors.'

In our studying of people we need a proper sense of perspective about ourselves as well as our congregation. We tend very readily to blame our congregation for any lack of growth and say, 'If only they were different!' Let us remember that our congregations may be saying, 'If only we had a different preacher!' Some readers will know another book in the 'I Believe' series, *I Believe in Church Growth,* by Eddie Gibbs. If so, you may recall his description of the 'ultimate chain letter' which apparently appeared in a number of Church of England parish magazines. It reads:

> If you are unhappy with your vicar, simply have your church wardens send a copy of this letter to six other churches who are tired of their vicar. Then bundle up your vicar and send him to the church at the top of the list in this letter. Within a week you will receive 16,435 vicars and one of them should be alright. Have faith in this chain letter for vicars. Do not break the chain. One church did and got their old vicar back!

We need a proper perspective about ourselves as well as our congregation, and remember continually this is God's work and in his sovereign will he causes growth and sometimes he withholds it, even when we seem to be doing everything right.

The title of this chapter is a constant reminder that preaching – true, biblical, reformed, evangelical, expository preaching – must always be rooted in reality. Over the years this one word has been a continual challenge to me – reality, reality, reality! Peter Marshall once advised men in Gettysburg Theological Seminary,

> You must root your preaching in reality, remembering that the people before you have problems: doubts, fears and anxieties gnawing at their faith. Our problem is to get behind the conventional fronts that sit, row upon row, in the pews.

He was surely right, for much of our preaching can be academic and theoretical unless we keep this in mind. So, who are the real people we are preaching to week by week? Let us consider the answer to this question under seven main headings to give some shape to our thinking on this subject.

1. Real people are our relatives

First, we must remember our solidarity with the whole human race, including that segment of humanity occupying the pews in front of us each Sunday. You recall how Paul began his great prayer for the Ephesian Christians in chapter 3, 'For this reason I kneel before the Father, from whom his whole family in heaven or earth derives its name'. The idea here seems to be the commonality of the whole human race under God. All hearers of the gospel wherever they are to be found, Timbuktu or Taunton, share the same basic needs: 'a man's a man for a' that', as Robert Burns put it. Phillips Brooks, in his famous book *The Joy of Preaching*, said he thought it necessary for a man to preach sometimes to congregations which he does not know, 'in order to keep the impression of preaching to humanity'. In preaching to any congregation we are looking the human race in the face.

We can become over anxious today about the need to understand the culture of our hearers or their sub-culture, or their sub-sub-culture, before preaching to them with any confidence. But in so doing we lose the fundamental plot of humanity, namely that all people share in the same universal common need – the need for God's grace. 'It is a vital part of preaching' said Martyn Lloyd-Jones 'to reduce all listeners to that common denominator'. There was a celebrated occasion, which Lloyd-Jones recounts, when he was preaching in the University of Oxford one Sunday evening in 1941. After the service a meeting was arranged for those who wished to ask questions of the preacher. The place was packed out. A leading member of the Oxford Union Debating Society asked a very erudite question, or rather made a speech, with the point that while the sermon was well-constructed and well-presented, it equally might have been delivered to a congregation of farm labourers. The Doctor replied by saying that he did not understand the questioner's difficulty, for he had up to that moment always regarded undergraduates of Oxford University as being just ordinary common human clay and miserable sinners like everyone else, and thus their needs were precisely the same as agricultural labourers and the whole human family!

All people share exactly the same elemental needs as members of the human race – the need for God and his gospel. Real people are just like us. I suppose that means that the word I preach to them is the same word which I find affects me as a real person. When preaching his sermons, Calvin apparently had in his mind one person in particular. Luther is often quoted in this connection: 'When I preach', he said, 'I regard neither doctors nor magistrates. I have my eyes on the servant maids and the children.' But there was, however, for Calvin always one man in the congregation at whom he directed his sermons and that was himself:

> He that speaks (preaches) must certainly testify
> that it is all in good faith, and that he has such a
> reverence for the teaching he proclaims that he
> means to be the first to be obedient to it... and
> that it is for him to make a start.

So if real people are like me, the preacher, I must know myself essentially as a sinner saved by grace. Calvin begins his Institutes by reducing all knowledge to two heads, knowledge of God and knowledge of self – and the two are related. Our basic aim is to teach people from the Bible to know themselves and God. How simple yet how profound.

But a caution here: by saying that real people are our relatives, I am not at all meaning that we should preach to them as though they were ministers! There is a real danger that we preachers tend to preach to one another. If we know other preachers are going to be present on a Sunday morning, we tend automatically to think of them in preparation and give the message a specialist slant (that is, what would appeal to them); consequently we lose touch with reality. Real people, on the whole, do not want to be like ministers! John Stott tells of a patient in the chapel of a mental hospital who, after listening for a time to the chaplain, was heard to remark, 'There but for the grace of God go I!' We have to recall the common need of all our hearers. Real people are our relatives.

2. Real people are flawed and fallen beings

We are sinners preaching to sinners, or to use James Denny's famous words, 'dying men speaking to dying men'. The more we handle the Bible, the more we know our own and other people's hearts, and we find that the Bible's truths penetrate even to dividing of soul and spirit, joints and marrow. The Bible really does judge the thoughts and attitudes of the heart. You cannot be a teacher of the Bible, or a preacher in any pastoral context, without being increasingly persuaded of the exceeding sinfulness of sin in your own life and that of others. Those listening, like the preacher, are facing weekly the fundamental conflict of the Christian life, the Galatians 5 conflict:

> For the flesh lusts against the Spirit, and the
> Spirit against the flesh; and these are contrary
> to one another, so that you do not do the things
> that you wish.
> (Gal. 5:17 [NKJV]; echoes of Romans 7)

Real Christian people are fallen beings, struggling continually with the good they want to do, but at times do not, and struggling with the evil they do not want to do, but which they sometimes succumb to. I suppose the longer we preach the less surprised we are by the outbreaks and expressions of human sin in the

Christian community.

Craig Loscalzo in a recent book, *Apologetic Preaching*, says that post-modern people today bring with them two presuppositions in connection with the Christian gospel. One is, 'It's alright to believe anything as long as I believe something', and the second is, 'I'm OK – you're OK.' It is very hard, says the writer, for post-moderns to hear, 'I'm a sinner – you're a sinner'. But that is where we must start, as that is where the Bible starts. But that is also where we must continue and go on until the end, preaching Christ as the Saviour for sinners. Jesus himself was the great *Kardiognostes* or heart-knower (Acts 1:24) who searches mind and heart (Rev. 2:23). We need constantly to seek insight from him to understand the subtlety of sin and its power, and to apply the solution of grace to our hearers. A good motto is the well known aphorism: the true function of a preacher is to disturb the comfortable and also to comfort the disturbed. Real people are flawed and fallen beings.

3. Real people are frail flesh and blood

'He remembers that we are dust' (Psalm 103). Constantly we have to remember that in relation to the people before us. I suppose people have always had to face pressures in their lives, but my distinct impression over the last twenty years is that the pace of working life is quickening and Christian people are under more pressure. Ironically, technology guaranteed us a better life by saving us time. What happened? Everyone has washing machines, dishwashers, ice-dispensing refrigerators, microwave ovens, waste-disposers, hairdryers, self-propelled lawnmowers, answering machines and access to information superhighways. Everyone has all these things but no-one has any time! Pressures are intense. Young men are retiring in their late forties and early fifties, ground to the dust. In the pressures of modern business and professional life it is very difficult to get leaders and other committed people to attend regularly at midweek meetings for prayer, or come to elders'/leaders' meetings, or participate in visiting homes to encourage faith, and so on. The New Testament is aware of the pressures of real living: 'We do not want you to be uninformed ... about the *thlipsis* we suffered' (2 Cor. 1:8ff.). Paul uses this noun, or its verbal form, four times in these four famous verses; the word is variously translated in the New Testament as affliction, hardship, troubles, trials, anguish, distress. Literally it means 'pressure from all sides' and can refer to anything which burdens the human spirit. It is a strong word. Think of the old wood-vice on a work bench. It had two arms which moved from different directions to clamp together and squeeze what is on the inside – that is *thlipsis*. And many of our people are having the very life squeezed out of them by pressures of all kinds in their work and personal circumstances.

As preachers we must be aware of these various forms of thlipsis. Real people are in church on Sundays looking for something to help them with their frailties, vulnerabilities and pressures. It is of the greatest importance that we think ourselves into their situations. Some in the congregation are probably convinced the minister does not understand their difficulties in modern business life. We have to be very practical in our teaching of the Bible. Calvin said in a sermon on 2 Timothy 3:16, 'When I expound Holy Scripture, I must always make this my rule— that those who hear me may receive profit from the teaching I put forward.' He obviously had no idealised view of the congregation as though all his hearers were wholehearted Bible students—the 119th Psalm personified! But he knew they needed help. THL Parker, the great Calvin scholar, interestingly detects a low-key presentation in Calvin's sermons in 2 Timothy 3 on the use of Scripture.

> There is no threshing himself into a fervour
> of impatience, no holier than thou rebuking. It
> is simply one man, conscious of his sins, aware
> of how little progress he makes, and how hard

> it is to be a doer of the Word, sympathetically
> passing on what God has said to them and to
> him.

Another indication of Calvin's own involvement in the frailties of his people is the almost universal use in his sermons of 'we' and 'us' and the rare use of 'you'. The preacher is under the authority of God's word as much as the hearers, and needs the same practical profit. In *I Believe in Preaching*, John Stott quotes someone saying that one of the preacher's tasks in the pulpit is to 'put heart into men for the coming week', and adds the words of RW Dale, the nineteenth-century Congregationalist: 'People want to be comforted. They need consolation – they really need it and do not merely long for it.' Real people are frail flesh and blood.

4. Real people are rational and 'affectionate' creatures

Lloyd-Jones used to refer to the order of human psychology as mind, heart, will. The word goes to the mind first, then through to the heart, and on to the will, in that order. That is God's intention for human beings, but as a result of the fall everything is reversed when impulses of the will and the power of the emotions lead the way, instead of the mind. The gospel seeks to redress the damage. So the real people sitting in their serried ranks on a Sunday morning are rational creatures in this sense, despite what we are told by all the post-modern gurus. Certainly, it is amazing in our culture how many people, who are intelligent and well educated in their own spheres, are extremely sentimental and can have their feelings aroused by the most banal story. Maybe Christian people are so exhausted with their work during the week, that they just slump on a Sunday morning and feel the need to be entertained, amused or 'moved'. But we must resist today's pressure to being merely story-tellers or anecdotal preachers whose aim is to trigger off some feeling and give people a warm dose of the 'fuzzies'. Real people need (and deep down want) that which is addressed to their minds and that which appeals first and foremost to their thinking powers. That does not mean a sermon should be an academic discourse. Absolutely not! But we should always take seriously the persistent apostolic injunctions in the New Testament which refer to hearing, learning, knowing, seeing, understanding and so on. It is precisely because we are preaching to real people that we must address their minds first and foremost in our preaching.

Preaching that addresses the mind puts a premium on clarity. My first sermon as a candidate for the ministry was critiqued by a university lecturer who was noted for his caustic comments. His first line to me at our assessment session was, 'Allen, your sermon reminded me of the opening words from the book of Genesis: "And the earth was without form and there was a great void". I got the message and ever since have tried to focus on a clear structure. Real people, whatever their social standing or educational background, need to be persuaded by a clear, plain, reasoned, structured and logical explanation of the truth. 'By setting forth the truth plainly [or clearly], we commend ourselves to every man's conscience in the sight of God '(2 Cor. 4:2). It is very hard work to aim for form and plainness when handling paragraphs which are complicated. But we must: real people want to understand what the Bible is teaching because they are rational creatures.

Yet as well as rational creatures, they are 'affectionate' ones as well. I use the word 'affectionate' in the sense in which Jonathan Edwards used the term in his classic work *The Religious Affections*. Edwards' point was that in biblical thinking the centre of a person's being was the heart, the seat of the affections, and the affections (much more than the feelings and emotions) had to do with the inclination of a person's direction towards that which was desirable and against that which was off-putting. 'Out of the heart flow the issues of life', and 'My son, give me your heart', says Proverbs. The affections then are the target to hit in preaching; we dare not rest content with striking merely the mind, though we must never bypass it either. Mind, heart and will are all involved in an inextricable way, and we must take this more seriously in our thinking about preaching than perhaps we do.

5. Real people are contemporary men and women

Evangelical preachers have been guilty of a kind of gnosticism at times. In our preaching on Sundays we draw people into the rarefied atmosphere of the spiritual world, and then they move off into the material world with their office work on Mondays to Fridays. But such a division of realms is unbiblical. Paul addresses his letters to believers where they are. For example, he begins the Colossian epistle by writing to 'the holy and faithful, in Christ, in Colosse' (not *at* Colosse, as in the NIV). This is a summary of a believer's life: 'in Christ, in Colosse'. Yet there has always been a difficulty for the hearers connecting life in Christ with life in Colosse, or in Glasgow, or wherever. Real people want that connection and need it to be made obvious. We have to work harder with our application and illustrative material to show we are preaching to twenty-first-century men and women in their particular culture.

John Stott is helpful in this in his chapter on 'Preaching as Bridge-building'. He recognises the perils in the clamant demand for relevance today, but urges us to take seriously the perception that many people have of a yawning chasm between the biblical world and the modern world. Faced with the problem of the communication gulf between the two worlds, preachers, says Stott, tend to make one of two mistakes. On the one hand conservatives are biblical but not contemporary, while on the other hand liberals are contemporary but not biblical. 'Why must we polarise?' he asks. Chrysostom is cited to show the combination of two qualities, which made him unique: 'He was a man of the Word and a man of the world – his message had both a timeless and timely element in it.' This analysis may or may not be correct, but at least it points out the real need for preachers who are committed to biblical preaching to ensure they are living and preaching in today's world. 'What do you do to prepare your Sunday sermon?' Karl Barth was once asked. He replied, 'I take the Bible in one hand and the daily newspaper in the other.' A century earlier, CH Spurgeon had written what he entitled *My Little Shilling Book; the Bible and the Newspaper*. Real people are not interested in the niceties of textual interpretation or the fine points of theological disputation. (That is work for the preacher's study, not the pulpit.) But they do sit and listen if you can show clearly the relevance of the Bible to what is happening in the weekly events of national and local life.

So I unashamedly ransack daily newspapers, *Newsweek*, *New Statesman* and TV programmes for relevant appropriate notes, quotations and anecdotes that put contemporary flesh on to biblical bones. I happened to be looking at a recent issue of *New Statesman* and saw an editorial titled 'This Selfish Land'. The first two paragraphs gave lots of examples of the essential selfishness of our society and culture as it has become. A modern counterpart, I thought, to the last verse of the book of Judges. Then came this sentence: 'It is the great failure of the Clinton administration in the U.S. and the potential failure of New Labour in Britain, that it has failed utterly to change the culture.' Well, 1 Samuel 13-15 could have told you that, Mr Editor, and a lot more, if you would like to listen!

We are preaching to contemporary men and women who live in the twenty-first century and we had better not forget it. I have sat in the pews at times and listened to messages which were undeniably biblical, but which could have been preached in the eighteenth or nineteenth centuries. But real people do not live in these days any more.

6. Real people are responsive humans

Because there are hundreds of books written about the preacher and very few about the hearers, the assumption seems to be that whereas the preacher is really doing something, the people have a passive role, like so many jugs waiting to be filled up. Just pour out the pure word into these jugs and they will receive it. But they will not unless they respond to what is being taught, and they will only respond, humanly speaking, if their interest has been aroused. We can bore our congregation to tears at times! We have to try to make our teaching vivid, graphic and colourful. If we understand real people we will know the importance of grabbing their attention from the beginning with carefully chosen words that arouse them to sit up and take notice. Spurgeon's *Lectures to My Students* are full of wisdom on this point. This quotation has stayed with me over the last quarter of a century more than any other from Spurgeon:

> God helping me, I will teach the people by parables, by similes, by illustrations, by preaching, by anything that will help them and I will seek to be a thoroughly interesting preacher of the Word.

Lloyd-Jones thought Spurgeon had too many illustrations, but perhaps he undervalued human responsiveness to illustrations and humour. Obviously too many illustrations can stifle the content, and can interrupt the proper use of tension in the accumulation of points in an argument. In the symposium *Preaching* (Ed. Samuel T Logan Jr), RC Sproul in his chapter on 'The Whole Man' quotes the businessman who says that there are only three significant factors that determine the value of real estate. The first is location, the second is location and the third is location. Sproul went on to say that the same may be said for clear communication: Illustrate, Illustrate, Illustrate. Here, I tend to beg, borrow or steal any illustration, although one's own are usually best. Illustrations must serve the point not detract from it. It is of course possible to allow anecdotes to take over, and we must resist this vigorously. But, real human beings listen, learn, retain and respond to things made pictorial. Illustrations are like windows in a house to let light in.

What about humour? Some say it is totally out of place in the pulpit; all I can say to that is that they must be totally out of touch with real people and their humanity and what they respond to. Of course there is gratuitous joking and frivolity that merely puffs up the preacher, which is very different from natural humour that serves the message. There is certainly no place for the former. But the latter is surely inevitable if we are going to be engaging and real. It is a cultural thing to some extent. Glasgow congregations, for example, are very different from those in Inverness, or London, and you recognise the difference and adjust accordingly. Stott has a helpful few pages on this subject in his book on preaching where he underlines our Lord's own use of humour as the master teacher. The value of humour in the right place, says Stott, is that firstly, it breaks tension (intensity can only be endured for a certain period). Secondly, laughter has an extraordinary power to break down people's defences. Thirdly, it pricks the bubble of human pomposity. So humour, yes, used wisely and naturally is part of being a real person yourself, and part of preaching to other real people.

7. Real people are eternal souls

Finally, and perhaps most important of all, we must remember the great goal we are working for. Calvin, while preaching a series of sermons on 2 Timothy 3:16 and the function of Scripture, decided to tell the congregation why he was in the pulpit Sunday by Sunday. I tried that out myself a short time ago and used Calvin's words as my explanation; I said it was a fair statement of what both I and the sermon were for. Calvin said,

> It is so that God may govern us and that we may have our Lord Jesus Christ as Sovereign Teacher, so that we may be the flock He leads.

The definition 'that God may govern us' underlines application; if we remember that real people are eternal souls we shall be strong on application. Packer's definition of preaching is 'teaching plus application' (i.e. invitation, direction and summons); he says evangelicals today are somewhat weak on application, compared with a previous age. We tend to end most of our sermons by exhorting our hearers in the last few minutes to trust the Lord, read the Bible more and keep praying, and that is it. The Puritans are often quoted as models of application; it is reckoned that as much as half their preaching time was devoted to practical and experimental applications. It sounds a lot, but it is not if we remember that our aim is not to stuff people's heads but to affect people's souls.

I suppose the ideal to try and follow is that epitomised by Jonathan Edwards of whom it was said, 'All his doctrine was application and his application doctrine.' Recalling, as we prepare our sermons, that we preach 'as dying men to dying men' will wonderfully concentrate the mind to focus more attention on the application of the message to the lives of our people, for the purpose of their transformation. Holding constantly in our minds the truth that real people are eternal souls will not only influence the content but also the presentation of the content. Our style should be natural. Real people see through unreality right away; they quickly spot professional poses and this becomes a real turn-off. Our presentation will also be lively. I cannot understand any preacher being lifeless in matter while proclaiming the glorious gospel of the blessed God. Spurgeon has a marvellous chapter in his *Lectures* on the subject of 'Gaining Attention', in which he bemoans the fact that preachers' introductions are generally too long. The introduction, he says, should serve the same function as that of a Town Crier who rings his bell, calls out briefly and gives notice.

If we remember that real people are eternal souls our presentation will also inevitably be serious in its overall ethos, notwithstanding humorous illustrative material. We need to take with the utmost seriousness the centrality of the apostolic priorities in ministry, as found in Acts 6:4, 'We ... will give our attention to prayer and to the ministry of the word.' I do not think there is necessarily any significance in prayer being mentioned first in the text, but what is underlined is that prayer and preaching must go together if real people—eternal souls—are to be touched. I have often been fascinated to note in the history of the church how time and time again God has used these twin priorities as practised by the church to awaken eternal souls in times of revival. Sometimes the prayer has seemed rather unspectacular, but it is vitally significant, as it accompanies the preaching. Jonathan Edwards, who knew plenty about the consequences of effectual preaching, said,

> Preaching without prayer is like a sword
> without a cutting edge, a well without water, a
> fire without flame, a corpse without life. Such
> preaching may please the intellect or entertain
> the hearers, but it will never save sinners or
> slake the thirst of sin-sick souls.

So we have to be serious about these things and show our people we are serious about them. Such overriding seriousness flies in the face of our modern laid-back culture, but so be it!

If we remember that real people are eternal souls then our presentation will not only be natural, lively and serious, but it will also be warm and gentle. This quality marked the character of the Lord Jesus. Did he not say of himself, 'I am meek and lowly of heart', and did not Paul write of 'the meekness and gentleness of Christ' (2 Cor. 10:1)? In this a disciple is not above his teacher. So Paul expresses to the Corinthians his desire to come to them 'with love in a spirit of gentleness' (1 Cor. 4:21), the very gentleness which is a part of the fruit of the Spirit. In all these references the same word is used for gentleness. If gentleness is to characterise all Christians, it is supremely necessary for preachers and teachers to exemplify this quality. We have to guard against the use of sarcasm, self-pity and resentment in the pulpit, and resist the temptation to score points off those in the congregation. 'We were gentle among you,' said Paul to the Thessalonians, 'like a mother taking care of her little children.' So we must be patient with our people and never lose our tempers or give up in despair.

Real people respond to the reality of love, and we will love them more when we remember as preachers that they are eternal souls made in the image of God, made for a destiny of one realm or another, and made to hear the call of God in the proclamation of the gospel of grace. Let me conclude with these words from Richard Baxter:

> The whole course of our ministry must be carried on in tender love to our people. We must let them see that nothing pleases us except that which profits them. O then see that you feel a tender love in your breasts, and let the people feel it in your speeches and see it in your dealings. Let them see that you are willing to spend and be spent for their sakes, and that you do it for them and not for any personal gain.

5
Pastoring Real People

Jonathan Prime

Three fundamental convictions about the work of a pastor underlie this chapter. First, the calling and gifting to be a pastor-teacher is a singular one. God's call to be a pastor is to be an under-shepherd of that part of his flock which he has entrusted to our care. A pastor-teacher cannot separate his role as a teacher of God's word to his people from his role as a pastor to them; they are inseparably connected. Second, the public teaching and preaching of God's word, by patient and careful instruction, is fundamental to the work of the pastor. He must work hard at this task and give it a large proportion of his time, so that people may be called to the obedience which comes from faith. Third, while the public preaching and teaching of God's word is fundamental to the work of a pastor, there is more to being a pastor than public preaching and teaching. This chapter is concerned mainly with examining this third conviction, but must be read against the backdrop of a pastor giving his priority to the preaching and teaching of God's word.

No church is made up of cardboard cut-outs, but real people of flesh and blood. They are part of the church, just as the pastor is, and just like him they breathe, eat, sleep, work and are tempted to sin. They fall out with one another, do not always like everything that is proclaimed from God's word, and share the common joys and sorrows of life. Any fellowship is a diverse group of people at differing stages of Christian maturity. Despite their diversity they will also have much in common as sheep in God's flock. Within that flock, each individual believer is loved and has been chosen by God. Each has trusted the Lord Jesus Christ for eternal salvation through his work on the cross. Each is tempted in various ways to sin, to give up and to stop growing in their relationship with the Lord. Each shares the characteristics of 'sheep' which we all share, including being stubborn, foolish and often wayward. All, therefore, need shepherding, pastoring – commonly described as pastoral care. However, the term pastoral care requires definition.

WHAT IS PASTORAL CARE?

A recent article in an evangelical publication quotes research which suggests more than half the evangelical ministers in the United Kingdom have considered leaving the ministry at some point because of the pressure it brings. Apparently 53 per cent of clergy and other church leaders have wanted at times to escape from the stress of their workload, and 38 per cent of clergy feel overwhelmed by the complexity of daily pastoral care. Stress is identified as the most common pastoral issue with which they are called to deal. This is followed by marriage guidance, bereavement, loneliness and depression. The researchers suggested that these figures invite reflection on how well pastors are trained to deal with psychological problems like depression and stress. The implication is that many pastors should be seeking better training and continuing professional support to maintain the delivery of effective pastoral care in such crucial areas.

Unfortunately the researcher's suggestion reflects a common misconception of biblical pastoral care. The impression it gives is that pastoral care is about meeting people's felt needs – dealing with problems and crises in people's lives by crisis counselling. But is this how the Bible defines pastoral care? I don't believe so. This does not mean that a pastor will not be concerned for, involved with and seeking to provide support for people as they encounter stress, marriage problems, loneliness, depression or the myriad of other issues which arise. However, it must be clearly recognised that the focus of the work of the pastor is not primarily on helping people with their felt problems. This was not the focus of our evangelical forebears. Richard Baxter, for example, stated that his aim in pastoral work was to spread the knowledge of Christ among his people by personal ministry. (Today we would call this discipling.) More importantly it was not the focus of the apostle Paul. Paul's first letter to the Thessalonians provides a model of pastoral care. He reveals his pastoral heart as he shares his concerns for the fledgling church at Thessalonica, and describes his attitude towards those for whom Christ died. Exactly how long Paul spent in Thessalonica during his second missionary journey we cannot be sure. But in this letter Paul describes how his pastoral concern for the Thessalonian Christians expressed itself both when he was present with them or absent. As such it provides a model for us to follow.

Defining biblical pastoral care

The following sentence is an attempt to sum up what can be learned about pastoring real people from 1 Thessalonians, providing a working definition of biblical pastoral care:

> Pastoring real people involves loving them by sharing our lives as well as God's word with them, so that they might live lives which please God, in preparation for the coming of the Lord Jesus.

First, then, pastoring real people involves loving them. This may seem obvious, but it deserves emphasis. It is right to be concerned when we hear pastors speaking critically and unlovingly about the people they have been called to pastor. The genuine love Paul had for the Christians in Thessalonica radiates out of this letter. 'We loved you so much that we were delighted to share with you not only the gospel of God but our lives as well, because you had become so dear to us' (2:8), he says, speaking about when he was among them. And when he was away from them? 'But, brothers, when we were torn away from you for a short time [in person, not in thought], out of our intense longing we made every effort to see you' (2:17). And then, after describing how his efforts to see them were thwarted: 'So when we could stand it no longer, we thought it best to be left by ourselves in Athens. We sent Timothy... ' (3:1). Clearly Paul had a genuine love for the church in Thessalonica. Every pastor must ask themselves if they love the part of the flock of our Lord Jesus which they have been called to pastor in a similar way.

Second, pastoring real people means sharing our lives fully with them. Paul shared not only God's word, but his whole life with the Thessalonians. The little phrase among you occurs three times in the first two chapters: 'You know how we lived among you' (1:5), 'we were gentle among you' (2:7), 'You are witnesses, and so is God, of how holy, righteous and blameless we were among you who believed' (2:10). As Paul describes his pastoring, is he describing someone locked up in a study all week, preparing Sunday sermons and other talks, appearing briefly to deliver sermons and then retreating until the next preach? No! As Paul pastored the Thessalonian church he was among them. He not only shared the message of the gospel, he shared his life with them, so they saw the gospel lived out. And so it was that the Thessalonians accepted his message, not as the word of man, but as it actually was, the word of God, which is at work in those who believe (2:13).

But was it to please the Thessalonians that Paul, Silas and Timothy shared their lives with the Thessalonian Christians? Was it so that they might be praised by them? In 2:6 Paul expressly says it was not. Paul shared his life so that they might live lives which pleased God:

> For you know that we dealt with each of you as a father deals with his own children, encouraging, comforting and urging you to live lives worthy of God, who calls you into his kingdom and glory....
> Finally, we instructed you how to live in order to please God, as in fact you are living. Now we ask you and urge you in the Lord Jesus to do this more and more.   (2:10-12; 4:1).

Moreover, the clear purpose of Paul and his companions was to prepare the Thessalonian believers for the coming of the Lord Jesus. So much of what is seen as pastoral care today seems to be focused on the here and now, ignoring the Christian's eternal perspective. The unmistakable focus of Paul was on the coming again of the Lord Jesus. For example, in 1:10 he describes Christians as those who are waiting for the Lord Jesus to come from heaven. As Paul pastored Christians his aim was not just to help them with the pressures of daily life now, but to prepare them for eternity. Remember, it was against the background of these believers' experience of severe suffering for the sake of Christ that he wrote to them (1:14). And in this context his prayer for them is that God would strengthen their hearts so that they would be 'blameless and holy in the presence of our God and Father when our Lord Jesus comes with all his holy ones' (3:13). He does not ignore the present, but there is a clear eternal focus.

What does this mean in practice? Three pictures from the family emerge from 1 Thessalonians, which are helpful in considering what it means to pastor real people.

1. The pastor must be a brother

To pastor real people the pastor must be a brother to them. In all but three of Paul's letters, he starts by referring to his identity as an apostle. That is not how he starts this letter (or 2 Thessalonians or Philippians). There are dangers in reading too much into an omission, but seventeen times in this short letter Paul specifically refers to the Christians in Thessalonica as his brothers. Surely this must be significant! Although the church in Thessalonica was relatively young Paul recognised every Christian there as a brother or sister. He saw himself as equal with each of them in God's family. That did not mean that he was unwilling to use his apostolic authority. He does so in 4:2, when he gives instructions by the authority of the Lord Jesus. However, his attitude was that of a brother.

Was this a lesson Paul learned soon after his own conversion? When God sent Ananias to the blinded Saul, he placed his hands on him and said, 'Brother Saul....' (Acts 9:17). What amazing words of acceptance for the man who had set out to take the disciples in Damascus as prisoners to Jerusalem. I have a physical brother to whom I am united by an unbreakable physical bond. He will never not be my brother. The same principle holds spiritually; I am a brother to every other believer in the Lord Jesus, united to them by an unbreakable bond. As a pastor I must never forget that is what I am to every member of the church God has called me to pastor.

So, writing as a brother, Paul assured them of his prayers for them (1:2-3). As a brother, Paul acknowledged that the Thessalonian Christians were as equally loved and chosen by God as he and his companions were (1:4). As a brother, writing of the evidence he saw of God's work in them, he recognised them as genuine believers in the Lord Jesus Christ (1:5-10). As a brother he was realistic in his concerns for them. In 3:5 he shows he was sensitive to the possibility that they may have given into temptation as Satan assaulted them through the opposition and suffering they experienced. Paul knew they were just like him and similarly tempted.

If we behave as brothers to those we are called to pastor we will avoid giving the impression that we are superior to them or above them. Remembering we are their brother keeps us from the danger of becoming a 'professional' Christian. We need to express our identity with the church family to which we belong: that we are equally sinners saved by grace, frail human beings who are daily tempted, and who therefore need the constant help of the Lord Jesus like everyone else. Pastors need the church family's prayers (5:25) as much as the flock need their pastor's prayers for them. Remembering we are their brothers reminds us to preach to ourselves before we preach to them. As we share God's word with them in a one-to-one setting or from the pulpit, we must also be applying that same word to ourselves. One practical point: it may seem a small thing, but it is wise to avoid thinking of or referring to the churches we are part of as 'my' church. It is not 'my' church – it belongs to the Lord Jesus. It is helpful to discipline ourselves to refer instead to 'the church to which I belong'. It helps us to remember that we are one with the people we have been called to serve. We are not separate from them.

2. The pastor must be like a mother

Pastoring real people means being like a mother. 'As apostles of Christ we could have been a burden to you, but we were gentle among you, like a mother caring for her little children' says Paul (2:6). What a helpful picture this is! But how it differs from the picture the world might give of effective leadership. Look at the words Paul uses: gentle and caring. There is some difference of opinion in the commentaries about exactly what the word gentle means but the picture is clear enough: a mother dealing tenderly with her young child. The word caring means basically to warm, with the idea of cherishing, nursing, caring for tenderly. Being like mothers we need to deal with the flock patiently, and show tender, loving care, especially with new Christians.

As a mother feeds her child with milk, so we need to feed new Christians with the milk of the word (1 Pet. 2:2) and to do so carefully at the pace they can take it. If, for example, we are reaching every part of our community we may have in our church fellowship those who are limited educationally. We have to think through how to feed them effectively with God's word, so that they are able to digest it. We need to speak much to our people about the Lord Jesus and his cross and all that is ours because of the cross. At various times the people we are pastoring will be like bruised reeds and smouldering wicks. We need both to speak of and to demonstrate grace and mercy towards them. Gentleness is to be a mark of our dealings with the flock, including those who oppose us (2 Tim. 2:25). This is God's concern; we dare not ignore it.

A danger for all younger pastors is to be so concerned to get things right that we neglect showing love for our people and instead continually tell them what they ought to do and be. A young Scottish minister was rebuked in the early days of his ministry when an older member of the congregation came to see him. After some flattering words about his first year at the church, the older man said the following:

> Yes, everything in the garden's lovely—or nearly everything. My boy, the garden is still waiting for the blossoming of one flower without which the garden of no minister can be perfect. I know we are not everything we ought to be, and no doubt we need a lot of scolding; but we'd all be a great deal better if only you would try sometimes, instead of lecturing us, to show us you love us!

The minister in question described these words as a turning-point in his ministry. Augustine said, 'Love me and then say anything you like to me.' Richard Baxter's flock used to say, 'We take all things well from one who always and wholly loves us.' Are we loving the flock entrusted to us, and letting them see that we love them?

Continuing the picture of the mother, we learn that like mothers we need to share our lives with the people we are called to pastor: 'We loved you so much that we were delighted to share with you not only the gospel of God but our lives as well, because you had become so dear to us' (2:8). Considering this verse has made me think about the relationship my wife had with our three girls when they were very small. The reality is that my wife shared her whole life with them from the moment we rose until it was time for bed. I am glad, because it meant my wife's life shaped my daughters' early lives; but it was a very time-consuming business! To pastor God's people we must give them time. We must share our lives with them, because this is part of the way their lives will be shaped by the gospel. There are clearly limits to the time we have available, especially as we have to guard the time we spend studying God's word for preaching and teaching. We also need to give time to our own families and we must be wise in our time management. But we do need to take time getting to know our people, their circumstances, and the pressures and anxieties they feel. We need to show them we love them as people, that we love being with them – including the young, the middle-aged, the old, perhaps especially to those to whom we would not naturally be drawn. We must avoid giving the impression that we are too busy to get alongside them. This is certainly costly: 'Surely you remember...our toil and hardship; we worked night and day in order not to be a burden to anyone while we preached the gospel of God to you' (2:9). Being like a mother to those we pastor will involve sacrifice. There are no regular working hours for a mother; it is unpredictable and cannot be tied down to 9am to

5pm. Who knows what the next phone call will hold? As we get close to people it may involve heartache as a result of sinful folly and backsliding, just as children may bring heartache to their parents. But real Christian people need their pastors to be like a mother to them.

3. The pastor must be like a father

Pastoring real people means also being like a father. While the picture of being like a mother highlights the gentleness, care and sacrifice involved in pastoring, the picture of a father highlights the educational role of the pastor. Like a father, the pastor is to educate his people. First by example: 'You are witnesses, and so is God, of how holy, righteous and blameless we were among you who believed' (2:10). Paul writes of the Thessalonians being imitators of him and his colleagues and of the Lord (1:6). We can only imitate those we observe. The sobering consequence of being among the people we pastor is that they become witnesses of how we live. Members of a local church are unlikely to be holy, righteous and blameless if we are not. To pastor real people we ourselves need to be growing as disciples of the Lord Jesus. I am grateful to God for a human father who has been a great example to me, including what it means to be a pastor of a local church. I am called to be an example to the people I pastor, as my human father has been an example to me.

Second, the pastor should also educate by individual instruction from the Scriptures. 'For you know that we dealt with each of you as a father deals with his own children, encouraging, comforting and urging you to live lives worthy of God, who calls you into his kingdom and glory' (2:11-12). The phrase 'we dealt with each of you' indicates that Paul is speaking here not of public preaching, but of one-to-one conversation in which the word of God can be personally applied. This is something we need to make time for in our ministries. Personal application of God's word can be done one-to-one in a way which is not possible in a public meeting. We cannot do this with everyone, but we can do it with some, and so, significantly, equip them to do it with others.

We must avoid thinking of pastoral care as focusing upon crises in people's lives. Verse 12 provides a model for pastoral practice: using the Scriptures to encourage believers (urging them forward that they might not give up, especially when various kinds of suffering for the gospel occur), to comfort them (consoling them with God's comfort, when they take hard knocks) and to urge them to live lives that please God. This is what Paul does in chapter 4. He spells out the practical issues involved in living lives worthy of God who calls us into his kingdom and glory—practical issues like sexual morality, brotherly love and honouring God in our daily work. This need not mean lengthy sessions with individuals. There is a place for meeting someone for one-to-one Bible study over a period of time; there is also a place for seeking someone out to enquire after their spiritual health. However, it must also be much more natural and spontaneous than that. It can happen as we meet folk in the street or chat to them after a meeting—taking every opportunity to use God's word to encourage, comfort and urge them on in their discipleship. What this will always involve is the pastor taking the initiative.

Of course, when we do help our people in a crisis, our aims are the same. While I regret the common misconception that pastoral care is only about meeting people's felt needs, I am not saying that a pastor should not be involved in people's lives when they hit trouble. He will be. Part of loving them and sharing our lives with them means being available in times of crisis to give biblical counsel, direction and even admonition. Say for example that a member of the congregation has been diagnosed as having an inoperable brain tumour and given only two months to live. It is not the responsibility of the pastor(s) to do all the practical caring required; others in the church need to be encouraged to provide practical care for families in such situations of need. But that does not mean the pastor(s) should have no contact with the family during the man's illness. While others look after practical matters, the pastor's role is to visit regularly in order to share God's word, pray with the dying man, helping him and his family to trust the Lord Jesus in their need. This is all part of being a brother, a mother and a father, seeking to encourage and comfort them from the word of God.

COMPETENCE AND CONSEQUENCES

Human parents have the responsibility of preparing their children for life. Pastors have the responsibility of preparing the congregations they serve for eternal life. What a privilege! What a responsibility! Who is equal to such a task? The pastor's competence in this – as in every other aspect of the work of a pastor-teacher – comes from God, not ourselves (2 Cor. 3:5).

From 1 Thessalonians it is clear that the kind of pastoral care Paul exercised had significant impact upon the lives of those he served. It led to evangelism as the Lord's message rang out from them and their faith in God became known to others (1:8). Paul expected it to lead to the believers sharing the desires he had for them for each other. He urged them to urge each other to be to one another what he had been to them (5:14). The task of providing genuinely biblical pastoral care is not a task only for the pastor. It is a task he must equip and encourage others to be involved with.

Eternal focus

The twenty-first-century world demands calculable success. The effectiveness of biblical pastoral care is only calculable by God. It is what He, not others, think that really matters. It is only when the Lord Jesus comes (2:19) that the fruit of pastoral labour will be seen. In the meantime the pastor may have the experience Paul describes in 3:8-9 of 'really living' when he sees those whom he pastors standing firm in the Lord Jesus. But whether we see such fruit or not, the challenge is to keep loving those entrusted to us, so that by sharing our lives, as well as God's word, they might be urged to live lives which please God, in preparation of the coming of the Lord Jesus Christ.

6

The Preacher as Theologian

Sinclair Ferguson

When I was a theological student, I came across some memorable words of Jean Daniel Benoit about the Genevan reformer John Calvin: he 'became a theologian in order to be a better pastor'. That may strike you as either interesting (a new slant!) or odd. If so it is because a principle that all of the Reformers (in England, Scotland and throughout Europe) held with great conviction began to fall increasingly into disuse from about the end of the seventeenth century: all biblical theology is ultimately pastoral, and all pastoral ministry is ultimately theological.

Think of the sixteenth and seventeenth centuries. Most of the theologians whose names we know were working preachers, pastors or bishops in some context or another. But then, for a variety of reasons we need not go into here, a dichotomy between the two functions of theologian and pastor-preacher began to develop. This has sometimes (mistakenly in my view) been excused by the apostle Paul's reference to 'pastors and teachers' (Eph. 4:11), as though these were two radically separated offices, not one. Thus we find ourselves in the situation in which it can be said of somebody, 'It is just as well he is teaching in a theological college, because he would be a disaster as a pastor'. Or, similarly, we say things like 'It would be a waste for him to go into the pastorate because he has so much to offer as a gifted theologian'. Of course our colleges, seminaries and other training institutions need our best minds; but not on the basis that theology is for the academy whereas ministry is for the church!

It is rare however to hear it said: 'it would be a disaster for you to go into pastoral ministry because you are not an expert in theology'. Yet do we not expect our doctors, dentists, optometrists to be experts in their field? Not necessarily narrow specialists but certainly experts whose understanding is way beyond that of the layperson's. Could it be that the relative lack of respect there is for Christian ministers among professional people (even those who are themselves Christians), derives in part from the fact that Christian ministers are all too rarely experts in the very field in which they ought to be, namely theology?

Why do I say that? First, because as pastors our whole ministry is necessarily related to being a theologian. But second (and here I can speak only for myself but perhaps also for others), because our theological colleges never taught us that principle, nor believed it. Consequently being a theologian has not been regarded as a good thing. Sadly many of my generation came into the Christian ministry having to do a quick crash course in teaching ourselves theology. The result is that there has been a great dichotomy in our thinking between what it means to be a minister of a congregation, a pastor of a flock, an expositor of Scripture on the one hand, and on the other hand a theologian. But this is a dichotomy that is not present in the Scriptures. The apostle Paul well understood as he handled the gospel, often as a pastor of a particular congregation (as in Ephesus or Corinth), that you cannot be a pastor without simultaneously being a theologian. Indeed, strictly speaking you cannot be a Christian without being a theologian (or, ultimately, a human being!). For the whole adventure and process of growing as an expositor of Scripture necessarily involves a very delicate relationship between two things: on the one hand, the system of truth that you have already discovered has emerged from Scripture (your doctrinal framework), and on the other, the fresh light that God is shedding upon that body of truth from the very Scriptures that you are constantly expounding.

Framework and text

Let me put it this way: there should have come a point in the life of someone going into pastoral ministry when, in a sense, you have 'bought the house' within which your Christian thinking will take place, develop and mature. The substructure of your understanding of the gospel is laid down, and the superstructure built. It has a certain shape, and is clearly recognisable as a dwelling to live in. You have the framework of your theology. But for the rest of your life, you will find yourself saying things like, 'We will need to change the curtains because they don't really fit'. Then, when you have changed the curtains you need to rearrange the furniture, and later you may want to renew the kitchen, and so on. The basic house, the system of theology, is still in place, but the whole process of living in the house involves an ongoing process of rearranging things in such a way that gradually your theology becomes absolutely coherent and self-consistent for you as the occupant. In a similar way our theology is constantly being reformed by the Scriptures themselves.

There are various ways in which you can see this at work in Scripture itself, particularly in the apostle Paul.

Unity of Scripture

First of all, it is implied by the principle of the unity of Scripture. The moment you go beyond seeing Scripture as a unity, to in any way demonstrating how Scripture is a unity, you have moved from the narrow exegesis of the text of Scripture to a theological formulation about Scripture, and drawn from it. What you are doing is recognising that there is a structure within Scripture that is coherent, that has its own inner logic and therefore provides its own inner system. Theology and exegesis, or theology and exposition, are going hand in hand.

Primary and secondary in Scripture

Secondly, there is a more obvious example of this from Paul at the beginning of 1 Corinthians 15. He says there that some things belong to the first rank in the gospel; they are 'of first importance', and he lays them out for the Corinthians (1 Cor. 15:3ff.). But that statement implies that there is a systemic understanding of the gospel in the mind of the apostle Paul so that he can say, within the consistent system of Scripture, 'Here are the things that are absolutely primary and principal; here are other truths that are equally inspired, but are not so close to the centre and the inner fundamental logic of the gospel.' This is not the thinking simply of an exegete of a text working through the grammar; it is the thinking of somebody who recognises that Scripture throws up for us its own theology, its own system of truth.

Paul clearly assumes that it is against the background of that system of truth that we understand how we relate one part of Scripture to another, and the whole of Scripture within itself.

Romans: a theological exposition

A third illustration of this principle is found in the way in which the apostle Paul expounds Habakkuk 2:4 in his letter to the Romans. He does a great deal more in Romans 1:18 ff. than simply give a grammatical exegesis or a running commentary on Habakkuk 2:4. What he does do is relate this text to the whole of Scripture and to the revelation of God in Jesus Christ. In fact the whole letter is the nearest thing to a full exposition of the theology contained in and implied by this verse, and this is what serves as the whole backcloth to the way in which he understands and proclaims the gospel.

The gospel pattern

This point is so important and neglected that it may be worth the danger of repeating it almost ad nauseam, so here is a fourth illustration. When Paul writes to Timothy towards the end of his life a new note is injected into Paul's teaching. You cannot really understand the pastoral epistles without grasping it: Paul is conscious that he has come to a hinge point in the history of the Christian church where it will be no longer possible for the people of God to turn to living apostles and ask, 'What is the word of the Lord for us?' In this context he urges Timothy to 'hold fast to the pattern of sound teaching' (2 Tim. 1:13-14). Note this: he is not to hold to the sound teaching merely (though that would be true). He is to hold fast to the pattern. Here typos refer to the mould, the shape of the sound teaching which in turn leaves its mark and character on our thinking and living.

In the process of doing this Timothy will guard the good deposit of the gospel in faith and love. What is Paul saying? As Timothy preaches the word (the principle to which he comes at the end of chapter 3 and the beginning of chapter 4) he must do so in such a way that his preaching is in every particular instance consistent with the good deposit, with the totality of that 'sound teaching'. So Paul seems to be suggesting that there is an intimate, intricate relationship between my understanding of the framework, the pattern, the consistent system of truth to which the Scriptures themselves give expression, and my ability to expound the Scriptures accurately and fully so that what they are for – 'teaching, rebuking, correcting and training in righteousness' (2 Tim. 3:16) – may be exhibited in how we preach them – 'correct, rebuke and encourage – with great patience and careful instruction' (2 Tim. 4:2 – the chapter division between 2 Timothy 3 and 4 must be one of the least helpful in the Pauline corpus).

I have used the word theology here in a rather comprehensive sense. Characteristically we think about theology in a multi-faceted way, the separate disciplines taught in our colleges and in the books in our libraries. In connection with our preaching we think particularly, perhaps, of biblical theology and systematic theology. In using the word theology as above I mean it primarily in both these senses: the teaching of Scripture seen along the axis of redemptive history and revelation (biblical theology as a terminus technicus); the teaching of Scripture co-ordinated in a coherent, topical and logical order (systematic theology as a terminus technicus).

It is clear, for example, that in his reasoning in Galatians 3 and 4 the apostle Paul is working, writing, thinking as someone who has a great grasp of systematic thinking rooted in biblical theology. For him redemptive history (biblical theology) is a handmaiden to the coherent ordering of truth (systematic theology) and this gives rise to application in the way in which he deals with the Galatian problem (pastoral theology).

This point; that the apostle Paul thinks as a systematic theologian to enable him to expound and apply the revelation of God to contemporary church life, presents us with a paradigm worth pursuing.

Theology: the expositor's essential anatomy

An analogy may help us here. Let me put it in the form of an axiom: theology is to the expositor of Scripture what anatomy is to the doctor in his consulting room.

When you go to the health centre and present your symptoms to the doctor, his ability to bring healing does not depend merely on reaching out to the current edition of The British National Formulary to find the appropriate drug. No, the physician's ability to bring healing where there is dysfunction (and herein lies part of the analogy with the pastoral task of providing spiritual medicine for the soul's ills) is intimately related to and dependent on a knowledge of the life-system that lies underneath your flesh. Furthermore, this life-system works in all kinds of interesting ways, because the good physician recognises that if you come with a pain in one part of your body the original source of the problem may lie elsewhere.

I remember going to my dentist one day because I had some discomfort in one side of my mouth. As I tried to relax (!) extended on his chair, he began to poke around in the other side of my mouth. Now, I had known my dentist many years, so once he had the tools of his trade out of my mouth I said, 'It is actually over here on this side I'm feeling the pain'. He replied that I had already told him that, but said that it could very well be a problem of referred pain – feeling the pain on one side, when the actual cause of the pain could be traced to the other side of the mouth. He knew that, given the complexity and interrelatedness of the anatomy of the head, the manifestation of dysfunction could be caused by a problem at some distance from, yet connected to the place where the pain presented itself. Because the physician understands how the physical body is connected and unified, how it 'works', it becomes possible for him to provide an accurate diagnosis and to employ the correct remedy to bring healing.

Diagnosis and treatment of spiritual dysfunction

While this illustration has its limitations, it nevertheless serves our purpose well. When you present your symptoms to the doctor, you assume that he knows his anatomy so well that he is going to be able to diagnose your problem and make possible the process of healing. Indeed if he or she lacked that acceptable level of expertise you would look elsewhere.

Should not Christian congregations have a similar confidence in us, their pastor-teachers, that we have a sufficiently clear grasp of the anatomy of the gospel, how it works, what spiritual sickness arises when we misunderstand, distort, are ignorant of it, or simply disobedient to it. To extend the analogy a little, they should be confident that we have a solid working understanding of the 'body of divinity' and how it functions so that we are able to use the remedies of Scripture to deal with spiritual dysfunction and foster spiritual health in the body of Christ.

This, again, is something that can be illustrated clearly in Paul. His letters, in the main, were written specifically to deal with one dysfunction or another in the churches in his care. His task is to bring to bear on this dysfunction the truth of God as it is revealed in Jesus Christ.

The diagnosis of division

Take his letter to the Philippians, for example. What is the dysfunction? It seems clear from 2:1ff. and 4:2 that the body of Christ in Philippi was beginning to present symptoms of a combination of divisiveness and mutual personal distance.

Paul understands the system of Christian truth well enough to see that it is simply not adequate to say 'You people shouldn't be falling out with each other, that's very naughty you know, you really ought to do better'. He does not preach moralistically to them, and simply command them what to do – to be united.

But that is often our reaction as preachers and pastors, is it not? We pinpoint the problem, and seek to bring redress to that specific area. We are heavy on noting the dysfunction and quick to recognise the proper function. We connect them by issuing a series of imperatives ('do this, and this . . .'). Necessary although this is, it is not medicine, because it is not gospel. It does not heal the problem at the root. And it is not what Paul does here. Instead he uses his theological anatomy. He traces the spiritual sickness to its real source, and understands the deep structure of the gospel and how it provides the remedy which will bring healing. In this instance the symptom of divisiveness presenting itself in the body of Christ in Philippi is traceable to the problem of pride. In that sense disunity is referred pain; pride is the root of the disease. Pride must be dealt with first, not disunity.

In addition, Paul also recognises that the gospel solution to the problem of disunity with its roots in pride must be found in the cultivation of humility. Thus in his thinking he has already moved from divisiveness not merely back to its antithesis in the principle of unity but to the remedial principle of humility. But then he moves on again, as it were, down through the anatomy, understanding that the source of humility in the life of the Christian believer is rooted in union with the self-humbled Christ and the imitation of him to which it gives rise as its necessary corollary.

Thus, the apostolic prescription for a return to spiritual health is a hefty dose not first of exhortation to work harder at church unity, but primarily an exposition of the person of Christ, exalted in his divine being, humbling himself to death, even the humiliating death of a Roman cross. The cure for disunity is Christology! And so, in the context of squabbles in this little church a perennial prescription is made out for Christ's people— a prescription which contains the most costly of pharmaceuticals: Christ's self-sacrifice in his incarnation, life and shameful death.

In this way Paul has done much more than simply give us the grammatical exegesis of the Philippians' divisiveness and then tell us it is an evil to be avoided. That would have been true, but neither adequate nor gospel. Rather he has taken his exegesis of their failures and placed this within the context of his understanding of the framework of how the gospel works. He has shown how spiritual dysfunction of this kind is inimical to the gospel; now he answers the problem with the grace of God in the gospel. He is dealing with the situation as a pastoral theologian, preaching not moralism, but grace.

The root cure for legalism and antinomianism

There is another dysfunction that is as common with us as it was with the apostle Paul. It is the dysfunction of legalism and/or its apparently antithetical dysfunction of antinomianism. In one form or another this accounts for perhaps 50 per cent or more of the pastoral problems we face. These problems may not surface with these labels, but in reality this is what is involved. In their relationship to God Christian people frequently fall back, in the most general sense, into thinking of their acceptance with God now being dependent on the works of the law. Or on the other hand, burdened perhaps by a sense of failure and the promise of freedom, they throw aside the commandments of God and the necessity of doing the good works that God has ordained for us (Eph. 2:10) in order to escape 'that kind of legalism'.

How does Paul respond here? If he operated simply at the level of symptoms he might well say: 'Oh we've got some legalism here. We're against that, and to provide a spiritual balance we will need a mild dose of antinomianism.' Or, correspondingly if faced with antinomianism: 'What we need here is a brief course of the law and its commands'.

Often throughout history that is exactly the way the Christian church has operated. 'Aha! Antinomianism: we need to tighten up a bit.' Or, 'Your problem is legalism: what you guys need to do is loosen up a bit; it is not so vital after all.' But that solution would be Freudian rather than Pauline! How, then, does the apostle Paul deal with legalism and antinomianism? Interestingly, he deals with both dysfunctions in exactly the same way: by taking both maladies back to the only lasting remedy for either legalism or antinomianism. This he finds in his understanding of the nature of grace, and the dynamic of the way in which it operates.

Take for instance the case of antinomianism, which he alludes to in Romans 3:8 as an accusation levelled against Paul's preaching and which he addresses head on in Romans 6:1. His response, if rightly understood, may strike us as sharply as a cold shower in the morning.

If someone in our congregation is a little fast and loose in their Christian life, clearly not living a life of consistent obedience to the commandments of God, would we go to such a person and say by way of prescription: 'You have been baptised!'?

Are we not more inclined to go to them and say, 'You need to cut this out'? But in doing so we become like cheats in Monopoly – we try to get past 'Go' without going round the rest of the board. We try to deliver them from spiritual dysfunction without reference to the remedy that was given to deliver us from it. We thus indicate our poor grasp of theological anatomy, of the structure of the gospel and the dynamics of its operation.

What Paul does in Romans 6, by contrast, is to take his readers back to the significance of their baptism, and the meaning of the grace we experience through union with Christ. He argues that all those who have been baptised (= Christians, Christ-ones, those united to Christ) have died to sin and been raised to newness of life. Certain implications follow from understanding the logic of this grace, and Paul expounds them: they are no longer servants of sin but servants of righteousness.

So where we may be inclined to take a short cut – after all is not Romans 6 difficult to teach; it seems so alien to the way we think today – the apostle Paul does not. He goes deep into the anatomy of the gospel in order to provide a permanent cure at the very root of the dysfunction – which is a failure to understand the truth ('don't you know' Rom.6:3,6) and to think it through into our mindset ('count yourselves dead to sin' Rom. 6:11). Notice the importance of the mind in Paul's teaching (both as to its content and its style). Understanding the radical nature of what has happened to us through union with Christ by God's grace is essential for the Christian; this in turn implies that the pastor-teacher must himself understand it.

The remedy for lack of assurance

Let me provide a third example. Perhaps it is not so true in England, but one of the great problems historically among Christian people in Scotland has been lack of assurance. Perhaps today we might be forgiven for thinking that there is not enough lack of assurance! Be that as it may, lack of assurance causes all kinds of harmful side effects in our Christian lives.

How would Paul deal with that? I think our native instinct would be to respond to it by talking about the doctrine of assurance. But the apostle Paul would probably have done that in only one case out of a hundred because he recognised that the problem – a lack of assurance and joy in the Christian life – is not necessarily caused by a flaw in our doctrine of assurance or the doctrine of joy. Rather, lack of assurance is almost always caused by an inadequate understanding of the free justification we have received in Christ and of the final standing before God that free justification guarantees to believers.

So Paul would not go to someone suffering from a lack of assurance and hand them a book about assurance; that would be an almost fatal mistake! He would preach the gospel to them: preach the freeness and the fullness of justification in Jesus.

Growing as pastors and theologians

Throughout Paul's letters, then, there is always operative in the way he responds to dysfunctional situations a crystal clear understanding of the anatomy of the gospel.

Remarkably, if we deleted from the Pauline corpus all the sections of gospel teaching drawn out of him by either dysfunctional understanding or lifestyle there is almost nothing left! He seems to have spent much of his time as apostle-pastor-teacher dealing with dysfunction. It is likely that pastors and teachers today will find themselves doing the same thing both in public and private. We therefore must learn to do our exegesis of the text of the Scriptures within the broader context of a constantly symbiotic relationship, in which exegesis feeds our theology and our theology enables us to expound Scripture in depth. Thus we grow as pastors as we grow as theologians. We grow as theologians as we grow as exegetes, and we grow as exegetes as we grow as theologians. And all this is in order that our preaching, our exposition of the Scriptures, may be truly pastoral and, in the biblical sense, theological. You cannot be a preacher without being a theologian, just as – in the truest sense – you cannot be much of a theologian unless you are, at heart, a pastor. How could it be otherwise if the chief end of our lives is to glorify God and enjoy him forever, and if the chief end of our preaching is that others should come to glorify him and enjoy him forever? And who would doubt that this is the chief end of our lives and our preaching?

APPENDIX

The Proclamation Trust

The main purpose of The Proclamation Trust is to encourage expository preaching, particularly among those whose full-time calling is regular preaching of the word of God. To that end we hold regular preaching conferences for ministers, and run our own full-time course, the Cornhill Training Course, preparing people for Bible-teaching ministries. PT Media seeks to make our resources widely available to those in ministry throughout the United Kingdom and across the world, through a large audio ministry, video training materials, website resources and the printed word.

PREACHING WORKSHOPS ON VIDEO

Even the most gifted preachers can learn together with others who share their calling, and preaching workshops can have a great impact on helping people nurture and develop their Bible teaching ability. These video materials provide resources for workshop groups among preachers or other Bible teachers. They can be used among ministers locally, students in college or within congregations to train Bible teachers in differing contexts, including teaching the Bible to young people. We hope they may help excite a desire to preach God's word as the answer to the greatest need in the church and the world today.

THE UNASHAMED WORKMAN: Instructions on biblical preaching

In Series 1, 'The Unashamed Workman', Dick Lucas distils decades of experience as an expositor into four lectures of 'instructions' that focus the approach to the Bible. Dick Lucas is chairman of The Proclamation Trust and Rector Emeritus of St Helen's Bishopsgate, London.

MEETING JESUS: Preaching from the Gospels

In Series 2, 'Meeting Jesus', David Jackman focuses particularly on preaching from the four Gospels. David Jackman is Director of PT and leads the Cornhill Training Course.

Each series is a self-contained, fully integrated resource with four video lectures, material for further group work, and guidance for leaders on how to set up and run a preaching group. Both use worked examples to illustrate basic principles of exposition, model it in their own approach to the text, and give further material to work through in groups to drive the message home. Each workshop set comprises the videos, plus the Leader's manual and one copy of the Preacher's Workbook. Further copies of the latter, which contains the lecture notes and guidance for workshop preparation, should be ordered for all members of the group. Further details are available on the PT website.

AUDIO RESOURCES

We have a very extensive catalogue of expository ministry, both sermons and conference addresses. Most is available on cassette tape, and selected materials are also in digital audio format (MP3). A fully searchable catalogue programme can be downloaded from the website, and there are also online catalogues in pdf format and as excel spreadsheets which are readable on most computers. Full details of sales and loan services are available online.

PREACHING CONFERENCES

PT runs about twelve conferences each year, primarily for those in full-time preaching ministries, but also for lay preachers and Bible teachers, students and wives of ministers. The largest by far is the annual Evangelical Ministry Assembly, held in London each June. Most of the other conferences are residential ones and involve work in small preaching workshop groups as well as main expositions. Details of all these, and booking facilities, can be found on the website.

CORNHILL TRAINING COURSE

The course runs either full-time over one year, or part-time over two years. It is aimed primarily at those intending to enter full-time preaching ministries, but we also have some places for those wanting to train for other areas of Bible teaching ministry, such as youth and children's work and ministry among women. Further details are on the website.

Details of all PT Media resources, conferences and the Cornhill Training Course are available on the Proclamation Trust website www.proctrust.org.uk

For further information on any of the ministries of The Proclamation Trust contact the head office.

The Proclamation Trust,
Willcox House,
140-148 Borough High Street,
London SE1 1LB.
t +44 (0)207 407 0561
f +44 (0)207 407 0569

pt@proctrust.org.uk
www.proctrust.org.uk

MEDIA

Other books from
Christian Focus Publications

DAVID JACKMAN

The Authentic Church

What are our
priorities before Christ
comes again?

A STUDY OF THE LETTERS
TO THE THESSALONIANS

The Authentic Church

What are our priorities before Christ comes again?

David Jackman

What are you doing between now and when Jesus comes back? Paul's letters to the church in Thessalonica are regarded as the first he wrote and so give us the oldest accounts of life in the New Testament Church. Paul and his colleagues took the Gospel to Thessalonica, where their evangelism was blessed in the creation of a thriving church. Despite this, Paul and his friends were forced out of the city, leaving the new church wondering how it would survive.

What are the most important things that Paul could write to them to keep them going straight?

He highlights evangelism, prayer, leadership and the use of spiritual gifts. He points out the problems with a misunderstanding of the second coming, the anti-Christ and what will happen on the day Jesus returns.

David Jackman explains all this as if Paul is writing to you, today - as we, too, look to be *The Authentic Church*.

David Jackman is Director of the Proclamation Trust. He is a popular speaker and is in demand as an advisor for pastoring growing churches.

'....when your Alpha course (or your home-made equivalent) is finished, introduce them to Thessalonians and use this excellent, easy to read book.'

Evangelicals Now

ISBN 1 85792 197 6

DICK**LUCAS**
WILLIAM**PHILIP**

TEACHING**JOHN**

unlocking the gospel of john for the expositor

Teaching John

Unlocking the Gospel of John for the Expositor

Dick Lucas and William Philip

Preachers find themselves turning to John's Gospel time and time again to proclaim its wonderful message about Jesus. This primer explores the main themes of John's own preaching of Christ, the Son of God, as preserved in the book he wrote for us. John makes clear his own key purpose in writing in chapter 20 of his Gospel, and this stated intention must guide the exposition of his words today. It gives a way into the text so the Christian preacher may expound the message as John himself intended he should.

Many commentaries are written on John, but few focus directly on the needs of the preacher and congregation. This book is aimed precisely there. John's own key is used to unlock 4 famous chapters of his Gospel from the preacher's perspective, and with the sermon in clear view. The goal is to whet the preacher's appetite for teaching John today.

Dick Lucas is chairman of The Proclamation Trust, which exists to train and encourage preachers in expository ministry. He is Rector Emeritus of St Helen's Church, Bishopsgate, where his four decades of ministry centred on thorough exposition of the Scriptures to congregations of businessmen, students and other young people.

William Philip directs the general ministry of the Proclamation Trust, including working with ministers and theological students, and overseeing the conference programme. Prior to entering the ministry of the Church of Scotland, Willie worked as a doctor specialising in Cardiology.

ISBN 1 85792 7970

Preaching the Living Word

Addresses from the Evangelical Ministry Assembly

Edited by David Jackman

Dick Lucas, Alec Motyer, J.I. Packer, Bruce Milne, Peter Jensen, David Jackman, Mark Ashton

'These superb addresses are the pick of the crop. They are absolute gold dust. I recommend this book enthusiastically and with joy.'
Wallace Benn, Bishop of Lewes

'This compilation of carefully edited addresses is an excellent sampler of the Assembly itself. More than that it provides the kind of instructive teaching and preaching which will serve to strengthen the ministry of the Word of God everywhere.'
Dr. Sinclair B. Ferguson, St George's Tron Parish Church, Glasgow

'This excellent book is a joy to read... it wonderfully captures the feel of the assembly'
Dr. Paul Gardner, Rural Dean, Hartford, Cheshire

In this book you will discover:-
 – How to make preaching more effective
 – How to restore it's centrality to worship in the Church
 – How to structure Bible exposition
 – How to preach from different parts of Scripture
 – How to preach doctrine

This is not a book about style, but how to extract the best from the Word of God when delivering a message.

ISBN 1 85792 312X

Christian Focus Publications

publishes books for all ages

Our mission statement -

STAYING FAITHFUL
In dependence upon God we seek to help make his infallible
word, the Bible, relevant. Our aim is to ensure that the Lord
Jesus Christ is presented as the only hope to obtain forgiveness
of sin, live a useful life and look forward to heaven with him.

REACHING OUT
Christ's last command requires us to reach out to our world with
his gospel. We seek to help fulfill that by publishing books that
point people towards Jesus and for them to develop a Christ-like
maturity. We aim to equip all levels of readers for life, work
ministry and mission.
Books in our adult range are published in three imprints.

Christian Heritage contains classic writings from the past.

Mentor focuses on books written at a level suitable for Bible College and seminary students, pastors, and other serious readers;
the imprint includes commentaries, doctrinal studies, examination
of current issues, and church history.

Christian Focus contains popular works including biographies, commentaries, basic doctrine, and Christian living. Our children's books
are also published in this imprint.

For a free catalogue of all our titles, please write to

Christian Focus Publications Ltd.
Geanies House, Fearn, Ross-shire,
IV20 1TW, Scotland,
United Kingdom
info@christianfocus.com

www.christianfocus.com